2009 EDITION

EXPORT PROGRAMS GUIDE

A BUSINESS GUIDE TO FEDERAL EXPORT ASSISTANCE

U.S. Department of Commerce
International Trade Administration

The Trade Promotion Coordinating Committee

Chair: Secretary of Commerce

U.S. Department of Commerce

Export–Import Bank of the United States

Overseas Private Investment Corporation

U.S. Trade and Development Agency

U.S. Small Business Administration

U.S. Department of Agriculture

U.S. Department of State

U.S. Department of the Treasury

Office of the United States Trade
   Representative

U.S. Agency for International Development

U.S. Environmental Protection Agency

U.S. Department of Defense

U.S. Department of Energy

U.S. Department of Homeland Security

U.S. Department of the Interior

U.S. Department of Labor

U.S. Department of Transportation

Office of Management and Budget

National Security Council/National Economic
   Council

Council of Economic Advisers

Welcome to the 2009 edition of the Export Programs Guide.

This comprehensive guide describes useful programs from more than 20 U.S. Government agencies that help U.S. companies export their goods and services to markets around the world. As many new and successful exporters have discovered, exporting can be an important source of growth, yet challenging. The information in this guide can ease this challenge by offering the support and assistance you need to become a successful exporter.

While the United States remains one of the most competitive and productive nations in the world, a relatively low percentage of U.S. companies are engaged in exporting compared to other developed nations. Although U.S. small and medium-sized companies with fewer than 500 employees make up about 97 percent of U.S. exporting firms, they represent less than 30 percent of the value of U.S. exports of merchandise goods. Furthermore, nearly 60 percent of all exporters sell to only one foreign market. Many of these firms could boost U.S. exports by expanding into other markets. In fact, there has never been a better time to export. Increased use of the Internet, improved transportation, and enhanced trade and investment rules have greatly simplified the export process and made it easier to sell abroad.

Exporters strengthen their local communities by creating jobs and new opportunities for American workers. This in turn contributes to the economic growth of the United States as a whole. If you do not currently export, consider it—especially since it is likely that your competitors are, or soon will be, selling internationally. If you already export, explore new markets. Either way, if you are new to exporting or are exploring new markets, the Export Programs Guide will help you understand the range of Federal export assistance programs. I applaud your interest in exporting and encourage you to partner with the Federal agencies listed in this guide to achieve your exporting goals.

Gary Locke
Chairman
Trade Promotion Coordinating Committee

CONTENTS

CHAPTER 1
GENERAL EXPORT COUNSELING AND ASSISTANCE

International Trade Administration, U.S. Department of Commerce

The International Trade Administration (ITA) is dedicated to opening markets for U.S. products and services and providing assistance and information to exporters. ITA units include (a) trade specialists in 107 U.S. Export Assistance Centers and 150 overseas offices, (b) industry experts and market and economic analysts, (c) market access experts, and (d) import policy and trade compliance analysts who enforce trade laws and agreements that provide remedies to domestic industries injured by unfair import competition. These ITA units perform analyses, promote products, and offer services for the U.S. exporting community, including the export promotion, counseling, and information programs that are listed elsewhere in this booklet.

Contact: For more information about ITA, call 800-USA-TRAD(E) (800-872-8723), or visit *www.trade.gov*.

U.S. Commercial Service, ITA, U.S. Department of Commerce

The U.S. Commercial Service (CS), a program of the U.S. Department of Commerce's International Trade Administration, helps U.S. companies—particularly small and medium-sized businesses—increase their international market share and sales. Through its global network of more than 1,700 trade specialists located in 107 domestic offices and 150 posts in 80 countries, the CS works one on one with companies through every step of the exporting process, helping them leverage world-class market research, promote their products and services in target markets, meet qualified international buyers and distributors, and overcome challenges and barriers that they may encounter while doing business in international markets.

Contact: For more information about the CS and its programs, visit *www.export.gov*. To speak with a CS trade specialist, call 800-USA-TRAD(E) (800-872-8723).

Trade Information Center, CS, ITA, U.S. Department of Commerce

The Trade Information Center (TIC), a U.S. Commercial Service resource, is the first stop for companies seeking export assistance from the federal government. CS trade specialists working in the TIC

- Advise U.S. firms on all government export programs.
- Guide businesses through the export process.
- Provide country and regional business counseling on standards and trade regulations, distribution channels, opportunities and best prospects for U.S. companies, tariffs and border taxes, customs procedures, and common commercial difficulties.
- Direct businesses to market research and trade leads.
- Assist businesses with the North American Free Trade Agreement Certificate of Origin and with other free trade agreements.
- Provide information on overseas and domestic trade events and activities.
- Refer businesses to local Export Assistance Centers as well as other state and local trade organizations that provide export assistance.

Contact: For more information, visit *www.export.gov*. To contact a CS trade specialist, call 800-USA-TRAD(E) (800-872-8723), fax (202) 482-4473, or e-mail *tic@ita.doc.gov*.

U.S. Export Assistance Center Network, CS, ITA, U.S. Department of Commerce

The U.S. Department of Commerce, the U.S. Small Business Administration (SBA), and the Export–Import Bank have formed a nationwide network of U.S. Export Assistance Centers (USEACs). Many USEAC offices are co-located with other federal, state, and local public-sector entities and with private-sector entities—making it easy for U.S. companies to find the help they need. USEACs are located in more than 100 cities throughout the United States and serve as one-stop shops that provide small and medium-sized businesses with hands-on export marketing and trade finance support. USEACs work closely with federal, state, local, public, and private organizations to provide unparalleled export assistance to American businesses trying to compete in the global marketplace.

USEAC trade specialists provide global business solutions by (a) identifying the best markets for their clients' products; (b) developing effective market-entry strategies based on information generated from commercial offices; (c) facilitating the implementation of these strategies by advising clients on distribution channels, key factors to consider in pricing, and relevant trade shows and missions; (d) providing assistance in obtaining trade finance through federal government programs; and (e) helping clients access state and local public-sector entities as well as private-sector entities.

Contact: For the address and phone number of the USEAC nearest you, see Appendix A, call 800-USA-TRAD(E) (800-872-8723), or visit *www.export.gov*.

District Export Councils, CS, ITA, U.S. Department of Commerce

District Export Councils (DECs) are organizations of leaders from local business communities whose knowledge of international business provides a source of professional advice for local firms. Closely affiliated with USEACs, the 58 DECs nationwide combine the energies of more than 1,500 volunteers to supply expertise to small and medium-sized businesses in their local communities that are interested in exporting. For example, DECs organize seminars that make trade finance understandable and accessible to small exporters, host international buyer delegations, design export resource guides, and create export assistance partnerships to strengthen the support given to local businesses.

Contact: For more information about DECs, call 800-USA-TRAD(E) (800-872-8723), or visit *www.export.gov.*

Export.gov

Export.gov is the U.S. government's one-stop portal for current and potential U.S. exporters. Export.gov consolidates export program and foreign market intelligence across 19 federal agencies and presents it under one easy-to-use Web site. Companies new to exporting can be guided step by step through the export process, and U.S. companies already exporting can view other guides, reference foreign tariff and tax information, search foreign and domestic trade events, subscribe to receive trade leads and industry-specific market intelligence, and gain access to federal export assistance and financing programs. Whether a company is exploring the possibility of entering foreign markets, searching for trade partners, seeking information on markets, or dealing with trade problems, Export.gov is the place to start. Additionally, the site links to federal sources of trade statistics, export documentation, financing, export licensing information, and much more.

Contact: To access the Export.gov Web site, visit *www.export.gov.*

Office of International Trade, Small Business Administration

The Office of International Trade (OIT) works with other federal agencies and public- and private-sector organizations to encourage small businesses to expand their export activities, as well as to assist small businesses seeking to export. OIT directs and coordinates the SBA's export finance and export development assistance. OIT outreach efforts include regional cooperative relationships with Brazil, Chile, China, Egypt, Mexico, and Nigeria, whereby the SBA's alliances with government agencies for small businesses in other countries are able to facilitate trade opportunities in those countries or regions and to support U.S. government foreign policy initiatives. In addition, OIT develops "how-to" and market-specific publications for exporters.

In September 2008, the SBA released the 4th edition of *Breaking into the Trade Game: A Small Business Guide to Exporting*. The updated book provides new and existing exporters with an international plan workbook and a complete guide to the basics of exporting. The guide can be downloaded from OIT's Web site at *www.sba.gov/international*.

In assisting small business exporters, OIT oversees the SBA's loan guarantee programs, including the Export Working Capital Program, Export Express, and the International Trade Loan Program. All of the SBA's export loan programs are available through USEACs and SBA field offices across the country.

Contact: To learn more about OIT, call (202) 205-6720, fax (202) 205-7272, or visit *www.sba. gov/international*.

Small Business Development Centers, Small Business Administration

Located throughout the United States, Small Business Development Centers (SBDCs) provide a range of technical and export assistance, particularly to small companies that are new to exporting. Such assistance includes counseling, training, and managerial support. SBDC counseling services are free to the small business exporter, but there may be small fees for export training seminars and other SBDC-sponsored export events.

Contact: For more information and the location of the SBDC nearest you, call 800-U-ASK-SBA (800-827-5722), or visit *www.sba.gov/sbdc*.

Service Corps of Retired Executives, Small Business Administration

The Service Corps of Retired Executives (SCORE), which consists of locally chartered volunteer organizations funded by the SBA, provides expert problem-solving assistance free of charge to small businesses. Helping American small businesses to prosper has been SCORE's goal since the program began in 1964. SCORE tries to match counselor experience with client needs and provide one-on-one counseling. SCORE also conducts well-developed, prebusiness workshops and a variety of business-oriented seminars and training sessions.

Contact: To learn more about SCORE, call (800) 634-0245, fax (703) 487-3066, or visit SCORE's home page at *www.score.org*.

Online Women's Business Center, Small Business Administration

The SBA's Online Women's Business Center promotes the growth of women-owned businesses. It offers programs that address business training and technical assistance and that provide access to credit.

Contact: To learn more about the Online Women's Business Center, visit *www.sba.gov/aboutsba/sbaprograms/onlinewbc/*.

Export Legal Assistance Network

With a presence in 70 U.S. cities and with the participation of more than 250 attorneys, the Export Legal Assistance Network (ELAN) program is a nationwide group of attorneys in private practice who have particular expertise in international trade and who provide free initial consultations on export-related matters to businesses that are new to export. Issues relating to export licensing, domestic and foreign taxation, tariffs, and intellectual property rights are just some of the topics covered. The ELAN service is available through SBA district offices, the Service Corps of Retired Executives, and SBDCs. For maximum benefit from the session, we recommend that exporters call ELAN after designing their strategic plan so they arrive with specific questions.

Contact: To contact ELAN, call Judd Kessler, ELAN national coordinator, at (202) 778-3080; fax (202) 778-3063; or e-mail *jkessler@porterwright.com*. The ELAN Web site is *www.exportlegal.org*.

U.S. DEPARTMENT OF COMMERCE

MINORITY BUSINESS DEVELOPMENT AGENCY

Minority Business Development Agency, U.S. Department of Commerce

The Minority Business Development Agency (MBDA) is the only federal agency created to specifically foster the establishment and growth of minority-owned businesses in America. The agency's mission is to actively promote the growth and competitiveness of large, medium-sized, and small minority business enterprises. MBDA operates the Minority Business Enterprise Center (MBEC) Program and the Native American Business Enterprise Center (NABEC) Program. These programs provide direct business consulting services to minority entrepreneurs, including access to markets, access to capital, management and technical assistance, and education and training. The centers provide entrepreneurial assessments and general business consulting, marketing assistance, loan packaging and other financial consulting, identification of and assistance in obtaining procurement opportunities, education and training, and various other entrepreneurial consulting services. MBDA currently operates 26 MBECs and 8 NABECs throughout the United States. MBDA works closely with the International Trade Administration on innovative ways to engage U.S. minority firms in the international business arena. Seminars inform minority firms of the tremendous opportunities available through international trade. MBDA supports several minority trade missions and matchmaker programs and notifies the minority community about all U.S. Department of Commerce trade missions.

Contact: To learn more about MBDA, contact Donald Powers by phone at (202) 482-7982 or by fax at (202) 482-3473, or visit *www.mbda.gov.*

A Basic Guide to Exporting, ITA, U.S. Department of Commerce

First published in 1938, *A Basic Guide to Exporting* is now in its 10th edition. This basic resource answers exporters' questions about how to establish and grow overseas markets for their products and services. Topics covered include

- How to identify markets for your company's products
- How to finance your export transactions
- How best to handle orders and shipments
- How to obtain free or low-cost export counseling

Contact: To purchase a copy of *A Basic Guide to Exporting,* visit *www.export.gov* or call (866) 512-1800.

CHAPTER 2
INDUSTRY-SPECIFIC COUNSELING AND ASSISTANCE

INTERNATIONAL
TRADE
ADMINISTRATION

Manufacturing and Services Industry Offices, International Trade Administration, U.S. Department of Commerce

Manufacturing and Services (MAS) is dedicated to strengthening the global competitiveness of U.S. industry, expanding its market access, and increasing exports. MAS undertakes industry economic and trade policy analysis, shapes U.S. trade policy, participates in trade negotiations, organizes trade capacity-building programs, and evaluates the effect of domestic and international economic and regulatory policies on U.S. manufacturers and service industries. MAS works with other U.S. government agencies to develop a public policy environment that advances U.S. competitiveness at home and abroad.

The Office of Manufacturing and the Office of Services have industry analysts covering virtually all industry sectors of the economy. The Office of Industry Analysis performs economic and statistical analysis to support U.S. industry competitiveness and evaluates industry recommendations for trade negotiations.

MAS also oversees key Department of Commerce Initiatives, including the Manufacturing Initiative and the Standards Initiative. Through the Manufacturing Initiative, MAS addresses the challenges facing U.S. manufacturers. Under the Standards Initiative, MAS coordinates trade-related standards activities across the International Trade Administration (ITA), the Department of Commerce, and other U.S. government agencies and seeks to remove standards-related trade barriers.

MAS facilitates formal private-sector advice to policymakers through an advisory committee program that includes the Industry Trade Advisory Committees, the Travel and Tourism Advisory Board, the Manufacturing Council, and the President's Export Council. Specialists are organized in the following sectors:

- Aerospace
- Automotive
- Building products and construction
- Chemicals
- Consumer goods
- Electronic commerce

- Energy
- Environmental technologies
- Financial service industries
- Forest products
- Health
- Information and telecommunications technologies
- Machinery
- Manufacturing
- Metals
- Service industries
- Textiles and apparel
- Travel and tourism

Contact: Trade statistics are available by industry on the home page of the Office of Industry Analysis at *http://ita.doc.gov/td/industry/otea/.* For MAS industry and international trade officers, call 800-USA-TRAD(E) (800-872-8723). To access industry office Web sites, choose "Manufacturing and Services" on the ITA home page, *www.trade.gov.*

Office of Textiles and Apparel, Import Administration, ITA, U.S. Department of Commerce

The Office of Textiles and Apparel (OTEXA) Web site at *http://otexa.ita.doc.gov* provides information specifically tailored to the interests of U.S. textile, apparel, footwear, leather, and travel goods producers and exporters. The site includes information on foreign regulations and requirements affecting U.S. exports, such as tariffs, taxes, and labeling requirements, as well as intellectual property protection and product standards information. Specific sector benefits and provisions under the U.S. free trade agreements are detailed, and relevant procedural information is provided. The Web site also provides information on trade events sponsored by OTEXA, as well as a database of U.S. suppliers.

Contact: For information on exporting U.S. textile, apparel, footwear, leather, and travel products, call OTEXA at (202) 482-5078, or e-mail *OTEXA@mail.doc.gov.*

U.S. Travel and Tourism Statistical System, ITA, U.S. Department of Commerce

The Office of Travel and Tourism Industries functions as the federal U.S. tourism office. Among its core responsibilities are the collection, analysis, and dissemination of international travel and tourism statistics for the U.S. Travel and Tourism Statistical System, as well as the promotion of international travel to the United States. Information disseminated covers

- Basic market analysis
- Survey of international air travelers (in-flight survey)
- Visitor arrivals (I-94 form)
- U.S. international air traveler statistics (I-92 form)
- Forecast of international arrivals to the United States
- International travel receipts (exports) and payments (imports) data
- Canadian arrivals and visitation program
- Travel Trade Barometer Program
- Travel and tourism satellite accounts
- U.S. Promotion Campaign

Contact: Call the Office of Travel and Tourism Industries at (202) 482-0140, or visit the home page at *www.tinet.ita.doc.gov.*

Trade and Technical Assistance, U.S. Department of Transportation

The U.S. Department of Transportation's Office of International Transportation and Trade serves as the department's overseer on collaborative trade-related initiatives and technical assistance programs. The office works closely with agencies such as the U.S. Trade and Development Agency and the U.S. Department of Commerce to organize business workshops designed to help establish relationships and share information between U.S. businesses and foreign officials who are likely to make—or heavily influence—awards of international contracts. Under mechanisms such as bilateral and multilateral agreements, the U.S. Department of Transportation's operating administrations participate in cooperative programs and technology initiatives with partners worldwide and promote policies that enhance U.S. industry access to foreign markets.

Contact: The following people can offer assistance: Greg Hall, Maritime Administration: call (202) 366-2765, fax (202) 366-3746, or e-mail *greg.hall@dot.gov;* Barbara Pelletier, Federal Railroad Administration: call (202) 493-6395, fax (202) 493-6401, or e-mail *barbara. pelletier@dot.gov;* Rita Daguillard, Federal Transit Administration: call (202) 366-0955, fax (202) 366-3765, or e-mail *rita.daguillard@dot.gov;* Juergen Tooren, Federal Aviation Administration: call (202) 385-8900, fax (202) 267-7179, or e-mail *juergen.tooren@faa.gov;* and Timothy Klein, Research and Innovative Technology Administration: call (202) 366-0075, fax (202) 366-3272, or e-mail *timothy.klein@dot.gov.*

Office of Fossil Energy, International Programs, U.S. Department of Energy

The Office of Fossil Energy enhances the competitiveness of U.S. industry by supporting project developers and exporters of domestic fossil energy sources (coal, oil, and gas) who are trying to expand their international sales of fossil energy technology, resources, and services.

Contact: To learn more, call Justin Swift, deputy assistant secretary for international affairs, at (202) 586-6660, fax (202) 586-7847, or e-mail *judd.swift@hq.doe.gov*, or call Barbara McKee, director, Office of Clean Energy Collaboration, at (301) 903-3820; fax (301) 903-1591; or e-mail *barbara.mckee@hq.doe.gov*. For the Office of Fossil Energy home page, visit *www.fe.doe.gov*.

State Regional Trade Groups, Foreign Agricultural Service, U.S. Department of Agriculture

State Regional Trade Groups (SRTGs) are non-profit trade organizations that participate in a program of the Foreign Agricultural Service. The SRTGs provide a broad range of programs designed to assist U.S. food and agricultural companies with the entire exporting process, from learning the fundamentals of exporting to identifying overseas opportunities and finding potential distributors. SRTGs can also help companies fund international marketing campaigns and promote products overseas. Their ultimate goal is to help U.S. companies build a global business. There are four SRTGs—one for each region of the United States.

Contact: To learn more about the SRTGs, call the Foreign Agricultural Service at (202) 690-3576, or visit *www.fas.usda.gov/agx/counseling_advocacy/counseling_advocacy.asp*.

CHAPTER 3
COUNTRY-SPECIFIC COUNSELING AND ASSISTANCE

U.S. Commercial Service, International Trade Administration, U.S. Department of Commerce

The U.S. Commercial Service (CS) of the International Trade Administration (ITA) helps U.S. companies—particularly small and medium-sized businesses—increase their international market share and sales. Through its global network of more than 1,700 trade specialists located in 107 domestic offices and 150 posts in 80 countries, the CS works one on one with companies through every step of the exporting process, helping them leverage world-class market research, promote their products and services in target markets, meet qualified international buyers and distributors, and overcome challenges and barriers that they may encounter while doing business in international markets.

Much of the trade-related information and many of the trade-related tools that CS offers are accessible through the Internet at *www.export.gov*. Companies can also call 800-USA-TRAD(E) (800-872-8723) to speak with a CS trade specialist about their specific issues. For hands-on, customized assistance, companies can work directly with CS trade specialists located in any of the CS offices around the country (often referred to as *U.S. Export Assistance Centers*). All domestic CS trade specialists are directly linked to their international counterparts (often referred to as *foreign service commercial officers*) in markets around the world, ensuring that CS customers receive the comprehensive in-country assistance they require.

International companies interested in sourcing U.S. products and services can find the tools and information they need on the Web site of the U.S. Commercial Service post—usually a U.S. embassy or consulate—in their respective countries. Alternatively, they can contact the CS post in that country directly. A complete listing of domestic and international locations and contacts is available at *www.export.gov*.

Contact: For more information on the U.S. Commercial Service, visit *www.export.gov*. To contact a CS trade specialist, call 800-USA-TRAD(E) (800-872-8723), fax (202) 482-4473, or e-mail *tic@ita.doc.gov*.

Trade Information Center, CS, ITA, U.S. Department of Commerce

CS trade specialists working in the Trade Information Center (TIC) provide export counseling and assistance on Asia, Western Europe, Latin America, Africa, the Near East, the Western Hemisphere, and the North American Free Trade Agreement (NAFTA). Country-specific counseling is available at no cost on country conditions; commercial laws, regulations, and practices; standards; government procurement; certification requirements; distribution channels; business travel; opportunities and best prospects for U.S. companies; tariffs, taxes, and customs procedures; commercial difficulties encountered in doing business abroad; and other market information. The TIC is the U.S. government's designated point of contact for help with documentation to qualify for NAFTA benefits and other free trade agreements. The TIC, through *www.export.gov*, provides extensive country and regional information, including a downloadable NAFTA Certificate of Origin, a tariff and Harmonized System number lookup tool, and contact information on foreign customs offices and trade offices in the United States.

Contact: For general information on exporting, visit *www.export.gov*. To contact a CS trade specialist working in the TIC, call 800-USA-TRAD(E) (800-872-8723), fax (202) 482-4473, or e-mail *tic@ita.doc.gov*.

China Business Information Center, CS, ITA, U.S. Department of Commerce

The China Business Information Center (BIC) is a comprehensive resource provided by the U.S. Commercial Service for small businesses that are interested in or are already doing business in China. The China BIC consists of an extensive Web site; a call center staffed by trade specialists; and a China seminar series, which is available nationwide. These seminars provide comprehensive guidance on entering the Chinese market and accurately portray the realities and challenges inherent in doing business there.

Contact: For information on doing business in China, visit *www.export.gov/china*. To contact a U.S. Commercial Service trade specialist working in the China BIC, call 800-USA-TRAD(E) (800-872-8723), fax (202) 482-4473, or e-mail *chinabic@mail.doc.gov*.

Middle East and North Africa Business Information Center, CS, ITA, U.S. Department of Commerce

The Middle East and North Africa (MENA) Business Information Center is a comprehensive resource provided by the U.S. Commercial Service for small businesses that are interested in or are already doing business in the Middle East and North Africa. The MENA BIC consists of an extensive Web site and a call center staffed by trade specialists.

Contact: For information on doing business in the Middle East and North Africa, visit *www. export.gov/middleeast*. To contact a U.S. Commercial Service trade specialist for this region, call 800-USA-TRAD(E) (800-872-8723), fax (202) 482-4473, or e-mail *menabic@mail.doc.gov*.

India Business Center, CS, ITA, U.S. Department of Commerce

The U.S. Commercial Service launched the India Business Center (IBC), housed in the Trade Information Center, in June 2008. The IBC joins the two existing business information centers—the China BIC and MENA BIC—in providing specialized assistance to U.S. exporters. The IBC's mission is to help U.S. companies take advantage of the growing market opportunities for export to India and to provide market intelligence and other information critical to the success of American companies in India. The IBC is also dedicated to helping U.S. companies overcome challenges to accessing the Indian market, including tariff and non-tariff barriers to trade, complex regulations, and infrastructure weaknesses. The IBC maintains a Web portal at *http://export.gov/india*, which groups all the information available about doing business in India. The IBC also provides specialized telephone counseling by trade specialists on the market and carries out outreach activities nationwide to raise U.S. business awareness of opportunities in India.

Contact: For information on doing business in India, call 800-USA-TRAD(E) (800-872-8723), fax (202) 482-4473, or visit *http://export.gov/india*.

U.S. Embassies and Consulates, U.S. Department of State

U.S. Department of State staff members advance U.S. foreign economic policy interests abroad and report extensively on the effect of economic developments on U.S. foreign trade and investment policy objectives. Foreign service officers (FSOs) provide political and economic briefings and advise U.S. firms on the business culture and practices of the host country. They advocate on behalf of U.S. business with key ministries in foreign countries and seek to build foreign government support for U.S. foreign economic policy goals. FSOs are responsible for commercial work in more than 100 countries not covered by the U.S. Commercial Service. They work closely with their CS colleagues worldwide. In those countries not covered by CS, close relationships between the FSOs and their CS colleagues are framed under the Joint CS–State Post Partnership Program.

Contact: For more information, call the U.S. Department of State main line at (202) 647-1625, or visit the U.S. Department of State's Office of Commercial and Business Affairs at *www.state.gov/travelandbusiness*. To learn more about U.S. embassies, visit *www.usembassy.gov*.

Regional Bureaus, U.S. Department of State

Country desk officers in the six geographic bureaus in Washington, D.C., maintain regular contact with overseas diplomatic missions and can provide U.S. exporters and investors with economic and political information from both a country and a regional perspective.

Contact: Visit the regional bureaus' home page at *www.state.gov/countries*.

Foreign Agricultural Service, U.S. Department of Agriculture

The Foreign Agricultural Service (FAS) of the U.S. Department of Agriculture (USDA) works to improve foreign market access for U.S. products, build new markets, improve the competitive position of U.S. agriculture in the global marketplace, and provide food aid and technical assistance to foreign countries. With a global network of 98 overseas offices covering more than 130 countries worldwide, FAS has the primary responsibility for USDA's international activities, including market development, trade agreements and negotiations, and collection and analysis of statistics and market information. FAS also administers USDA's export credit guarantee and food aid programs, and it helps increase income and food availability in developing nations by mobilizing expertise for agriculturally led economic growth.

Contact: Call FAS's Office of Trade Programs at (202) 690-3576, or visit the FAS home page at *www.fas.usda.gov*.

Platinum Key Service, CS, ITA, U.S. Department of Commerce

Through the Platinum Key Service, a program of the U.S. Commercial Service, U.S. businesses can attain comprehensive, customized support on a range of issues for which they need longer-term, sustained assistance. The service is solution oriented and tailored to the client's needs through a mutually agreed-upon scope of work. Assistance may include, but is not limited to, identifying markets, launching products, developing major project opportunities and providing government tender support, helping to reduce market access barriers, and providing assistance on regulatory or technical standards matters. Ongoing service is available for six months, one year, or a specified time frame based on the mutually agreed-upon scope of work.

Contact: For more information on the Platinum Key Service, contact the CS trade specialist at your local USEAC. For the address and phone number of the USEAC nearest you, see Appendix A.

Market Research, CS, ITA, U.S. Department of Commerce

Market research reports generated by the U.S. Commercial Service cover current conditions in specific country markets and identify upcoming opportunities for generating sales. These reports are produced overseas by in-country experts and are available at no cost to U.S. companies.

Contact: For more information on CS Market Research, contact the CS trade specialist at your local USEAC. For the address and phone number of the USEAC nearest you, see Appendix A.

Export.gov Market Research Library, CS, ITA, U.S. Department of Commerce

The Export.gov Market Research Library allows you to plan your market entry the right way—by using market research to learn your product's potential in a given market, your company's best prospects for success, and the market's business practices before you first export. If you are just beginning to sell internationally, you should narrow your focus to no more than two or three best-prospect markets. Use the step-by-step guidelines in the U.S. Commercial Service's Market Research Library to get started.

The Market Research Library contains more than 100,000 industry- and country-specific market reports, authored by CS specialists working in overseas posts. These reports include the Country Commercial Guides (CCGs)—annually updated guides to doing business in more than 120 countries that include information about market conditions, best export prospects, export financing, distributors, and legal and cultural issues. Also available in the Market Research Library are

- Industry overviews
- Market updates
- Multilateral development bank reports
- Best markets
- Industry and regional reports

To access the Market Research Library,

- Go to the Market Research home page on Export.gov: *www.export.gov/mrktresearch*.
- Click on the blue link to the Market Research Library in the third paragraph on that page. The Market Research Library page will open.
- Use the dropdown menus on the Market Research Library page to select the specific industry, region, country, or report type that you wish to access.
- Use the Date Range box to choose the time frame you wish to search for. For CCGs, which are updated annually, it is recommended that you search from the previous year to the current year to ensure that you access the latest report. For other types of reports, you may wish to extend the date range to cover earlier years.

Registration, which is free, will be necessary to access the documents.

Contact: If you need additional help accessing reports in the Market Research Library, contact the CS Trade Information Center at 800-USA-TRAD(E) (800-872-8723).

Customized Market Research, CS, ITA, U.S. Department of Commerce

Customized market research (CMR) generated by the U.S. Commercial Service produces individual responses to questions and issues related to a client's specific product or service. The research can address issues such as overall marketability of the product, key competitors, prices of comparable products, customary distribution and promotion practices, trade barriers, and potential business partners. Fees depend on the scope of work.

Contact: For more information on CMR, contact the CS trade specialist at your local USEAC. For the address and phone number of the USEAC nearest you, see Appendix A.

International Company Profile, CS, ITA, U.S. Department of Commerce

The International Company Profile (ICP) program of the U.S. Commercial Service checks the reputation, reliability, and financial status of a prospective trading partner. A U.S. exporter can obtain this information and detailed answers to specific questions about the prospective partner in a confidential report. Fees depend on the scope of work.

Contact: For more information on the ICP program, contact the CS trade specialist at your local USEAC. For the address and phone number of the USEAC nearest you, see Appendix A.

Videoconferencing Programs, CS, ITA, U.S. Department of Commerce

These cost-effective video services offered by the U.S. Commercial Service help U.S. companies assess overseas markets or overseas business contacts before venturing abroad. Companies can use these programs to interview international contacts, obtain a briefing from overseas industry specialists on prospects and opportunities, or develop a custom solution to their international business needs.

- *Virtual Trade Mission*. This service provides meetings with prescreened international firms by way of videoconferencing without the cost of traveling overseas. The Virtual Trade Mission focuses on your specific industry and allows you to meet potential partners and get answers to your market questions in an interactive videoconference.
- *Video Gold Key*. This service helps firms identify and meet with prescreened international firms. It includes three to five scheduled meetings with potential business partners and an industry briefing with seasoned trade professionals. All meetings take place through videoconference. Prices vary according to location.
- *Video Market Briefing*. This service provides time-sensitive market research for specific products and services. Benefits include a market-entry evaluation and a written report, followed by a videoconference with an industry professional so a firm can get immediate answers to market questions. Prices vary according to location.

Contact: For more information on videoconferencing programs, contact the CS trade specialist at your local USEAC. For the address and phone number of the USEAC nearest you, see Appendix A.

Featured U.S. Exporters, CS, ITA, U.S. Department of Commerce

The Featured U.S. Exporters (FUSE) service is an online directory of U.S. products and services featured on U.S. Commercial Service Web sites around the world. FUSE gives U.S. companies an opportunity to reach prospects online through a company profile in the language of the target market. Local distributors, buyers, and agents view company profiles. Leads are qualified by the local CS office and then sent to the U.S. company. Fees depend on the number of markets selected and translation requirements.

Contact: For more information on the FUSE online directory service, call Laura McCall at (206) 553-5615, extension 226; e-mail *Laura.McCall@mail.doc.gov*, or visit *www.buyusa.gov/home/fuse.html*.

Commercial News USA, CS, ITA, U.S. Department of Commerce

Commercial News USA, the premier export promotion magazine of the U.S. government, is published bimonthly by the U.S. Commercial Service through its private-sector partner ThinkGlobal. The magazine of U.S. goods and services is distributed (free of charge) to 105,000 prescreened potential buyers and partners in 176 countries.

Contact: For information on advertising in *Commercial News USA*, contact the U.S Commercial Service at 800-USA-TRAD(E) (800-872-8723), or contact ThinkGlobal at (800) 581-8533. You can visit the magazine's Web sites at *www.export.gov/cnusa* and *www.thinkglobal.us*.

ELECTRONIC MATCHMAKING AND TRADE CONTACTS PROGRAMS

The Export Yellow Pages, ITA, U.S. Department of Commerce

The Export Yellow Pages is used by foreign buyers as a reference tool to find U.S. goods and services. This service enables U.S. firms to present their products to a worldwide audience at no cost. U.S. firms can register their business profiles for free at *www.myexports.com*. Export intermediaries such as freight forwarders, sales agents, and other service firms that facilitate export business can also register their business profiles free at *www.myexports.com* in the U.S. Trade Assistance Directory, which is available online and as a supplement within the printed version of *The Export Yellow Pages*.

This program is a public–private partnership between the U.S. Department of Commerce's Manufacturing and Services Unit and Global Publishers LLC of Milwaukee, Wisconsin.

Contact: To register your business profile, call (877) 390-2629, or visit *www.myexports.com*. To receive a free copy of *The Export Yellow Pages* and information on other export programs, contact your local USEAC. For the address and phone number of the USEAC nearest you, see Appendix A.

Trade Leads, CS, ITA, U.S. Department of Commerce

Trade Leads, a service of the U.S. Commercial Service, provides U.S. companies with current sales leads from international firms and foreign governments seeking to buy or represent U.S. products and services.

Contact: Trade Leads is accessible at *www.export.gov/*.

Trade Mission OnLine, Small Business Administration

Trade Mission OnLine is a searchable database of U.S. small businesses that wish to export their products for use by foreign firms and of U.S. small businesses that seek U.S. partners or suppliers for trade-related activity. The database is designed to facilitate international small business sales, franchising, joint ventures, and licensing. The Trade Mission OnLine program is also used by the U.S. Small Business Administration (SBA) to recruit and provide time-sensitive trade promotion information to registered companies.

Contact: To learn more about or register with Trade Mission OnLine, visit *www.sba.gov/ international*. To contact the U.S. Small Business Administration, Office of International Trade, call (202) 205-6720, or fax (202) 205-7272.

ELECTRONIC AND PUBLISHED MARKET INFORMATION

Trade and Industry Information, Manufacturing and Services, ITA, U.S. Department of Commerce

The Office of Trade and Industry Information (OTII) provides comprehensive U.S. foreign trade and related international economic data useful in market research. OTII also evaluates trends in U.S. exports and imports by major product categories and foreign markets. OTII supports the data needs of U.S. trade negotiators as well as U.S. companies and organizations involved in exporting. The OTII Web site includes national trade and industry statistics, state and local trade data, and links to key foreign country data sources.

Highlights include

- *Exports from U.S. Metropolitan Areas.* Introduced in January 2008, this data series details U.S. merchandise export values by metropolitan area. The complete data series is located at *www.trade.gov/metrodata*. This new resource reveals that exports are having a positive effect on metropolitan economies.

- *TradeStats Express.* Located at *http://tse.export.gov*, TradeStats Express allows you to access the latest annual and quarterly trade data. You can customize, print, and download your own reports analyzing national trade data or state export data.

Contact: For more information and assistance, call OTII at (202) 482-5097, fax (202) 482-4614, or visit *www.trade.gov/tradestats*.

STAT-USA is the federal government's premier program for the publication of market information, trade leads, and other trade-related data, including the following electronic products:

- **STAT-USA/Internet.** Trade, economic, and business information is available on the Internet at *www.stat-usa.gov*. Thousands of international market reports and U.S. economic indicators from more than 40 different federal agencies are at your fingertips in an easy-to-navigate online database. STAT-USA/Internet provides current business trade and procurement leads, timely economic statistics, and valuable international resources and contacts all in one convenient location. Information that would take hours to compile individually is available in minutes. Subscriptions to STAT-USA/Internet are $75 for three months or $200 for one year of unlimited access. STAT-USA/Internet may also be accessed at no charge at more than 1,100 federal depository libraries nationwide. Subscribe online at *www.stat-usa.gov*.

- **USA Trade Online.** How many parachutes does the United States export to France? How many circuit boards does the United States import, and what percentage comes from Asia? USA Trade *Online* can tell you. This service provides U.S. import and export statistics for more than 18,000 commodities traded worldwide and the most current merchandise trade statistics available in a dynamic spreadsheet format. Using the statistics generated by the Foreign Trade Division of the U.S. Census Bureau and available through STAT-USA, USA Trade *Online* offers the immediate delivery of current and historical numbers 24 hours a day and the ability to manipulate data, store queries, and make charts. USA Trade *Online* is available on the Internet at $75 per month or $300 for an annual subscription. Subscribe online at *www.usatradeonline.gov*. To find a federal depository library near you, visit *www.gpoaccess.gov/libraries.html*.

For more information about these programs, call 800-STAT-USA (800-782-8872) or (202) 482-1986, or fax (202) 482-2164.

The National Technical Information Service (NTIS) is a source for government-sponsored U.S. and global scientific, technical, engineering, and business information. NTIS offers a wide variety of export and international trade resources, including the U.S. Trade Regulations and the Country Commercial Guides. To view the many products offered by NTIS, visit the NTIS home page at *www.ntis.gov*.

Contact: To contact the NTIS Sales Desk, call 800-553-NTIS (800-553-6847) or (703) 605-6000.

International Data Base, U.S. Census Bureau, U.S. Department of Commerce

The International Programs Center compiles and maintains up-to-date global demographic and social information for all countries in its International Data Base (IDB), which is available to U.S. companies seeking to identify potential markets overseas.

Contact: For information on the IDB, call 301-763-INFO (301-763-4636) or (800) 923-8282. For online access and free downloading of the IDB, visit *www.census.gov/ipc/www/idb/*.

Export and Import Trade Statistics, U.S. Census Bureau, U.S. Department of Commerce

The U.S. Census Bureau provides a broad and comprehensive range of foreign trade statistics that are available on a monthly, annual, and historical basis. The statistics cover more than 20,000 products, 240 trading partners, 50 states and territories, 45 districts, and 400 ports. Statistics include quantities, values, and shipping weights; methods of transportation (air, vessel, or containerized vessel); unit prices; and market share. These foreign trade data can be provided in different formats to suit your needs. Whether you are looking for data by product, country, state, port, or transportation method, the U.S. Census Bureau can help you. U.S. export and import trade data is available online at *www.census.gov* or *www.usatradeonline.gov*.

Contact: For more information, call Maria Iseman, Data Dissemination Branch, at (301) 763-2311; fax (301) 763-4962; e-mail *ftd.data.dissemination@census.gov*; or visit the Foreign Trade Division's home page at *www.census.gov/trade*.

SBA Internet, Small Business Administration

The SBA home page on the Internet provides SBA services, downloadable files, services from agency resource partners, links to other federal and state governments, and direct connections to additional outside resources. Special areas of interest focus on assisting U.S. small companies that are establishing new operations, seeking financing, looking to expand, and beginning to engage in exporting. The SBA home page also contains information on SBA programs that assist minority- and women-owned businesses. In addition, large libraries of business-focused shareware, downloadable SBA loan forms, and agency publications are available. A wide variety of services listed by state is provided, including local training courses sponsored by SBA. Online workshops are offered for individuals to work through self-paced activities that help them start and expand their businesses. In addition, the home page links directly to the White House home page (*www.whitehouse.gov*) and the U.S. Business Advisor (*www.business.gov*), which contain a large volume of regulatory information for small businesses. The SBA site provides full-text search capabilities as well as an area for user comments and suggestions.

Contact: For more information, visit SBA's home page at *www.sba.gov*.

Foreign Labor Trends, U.S. Department of Labor

The *Foreign Labor Trends* (FLT) report series provides a comprehensive country summary of labor data and labor trends in selected countries published by the Office of International Relations. The reports describe and analyze host countries' labor institutions, practices, and key recent developments. The FLT reports contain information on internationally recognized worker rights for bilateral or regional free trade agreements. The office also publishes the *U.S. Labor Profile* in English and Spanish.

Contact: You can visit the FLT Web site at *www.dol.gov/ilab/media/reports/flt/main.htm.* For more information, call Sudha K. Haley, Office of International Relations, at (202) 693-4801; or e-mail *haley-sudha@dol.gov.* For the *U.S. Labor Profile* (Spanish version), call Chantenia Gay at (202) 693-4906, or e-mail *gay.chantenia@dol.gov.*

CHAPTER 5
MAKING CONTACTS THROUGH TRADE PROMOTION EVENTS

U.S. Export Pavilion

The U.S. Export Pavilion is a multi–U.S. government agency trade show exhibit at major venues throughout the United States each year. The U.S. Export Pavilion promotes the benefit of exporting and of using U.S. government export assistance. Participating agencies include the Foreign Trade Division of the U.S. Census Bureau, the U.S. Department of Commerce's Commercial Service (CS), and the Export–Import Bank. In addition to those U.S. government agencies, the National Customs Brokers and Forwarders Association of America also participates by helping companies find a customs broker or freight forwarder in their area. Together, these participants focus on export education and on helping U.S. companies to

- Research export markets.
- Find international buyers.
- Comply with export regulations.
- Finance international buyers.
- Ship products overseas.

Contact: For information on the U.S. Export Pavilion, call the Marketing and Communications Office of the CS at (202) 482-0871.

Regional Promotions, CS, International Trade Administration, U.S. Department of Commerce

The U.S. Commercial Service of the International Trade Administration (ITA) maintains a number of Web sites that provide regional information:

- *Asia Now.* The Asia Now Web site brings together the resources of CS offices in 14 Asia–Pacific markets and of U.S. Export Assistance Centers throughout the United States. The Web site provides companies with a single point of access to regional trade events, extensive services, and research covering Asian markets. The home page is *www. buyusa.gov/asianow/.*

- **Trade Americas.** The Trade Americas Web site brings together the resources of CS offices in 21 markets throughout the region, providing companies with a single point of access to regional trade events, extensive services, and research covering markets throughout the region. The Web site also provides information on the existing and proposed free trade agreements throughout the region, market research, best prospects in the region, trade event lists, industry-specific information, business service providers, useful links, and key contacts. The home page is *www.buyusa.gov/americas/*.

- **Showcase Europe.** The Showcase Europe Web site provides a framework for coordination and cooperation among the U.S. Department of Commerce's CS offices throughout Europe. Organized around eight key sectors (aerospace, automotive, energy and power generation, environmental technologies, information and communication technologies, medical and pharmaceutical, safety and security, and travel and tourism), Showcase Europe provides market briefing and counseling at major trade shows through a team of market and industry specialists from the CS. Technical assistance focuses on identifying specific high-potential export markets for U.S. participants. There is no fee for U.S. trade event participants. The home page is *www.buyusa.gov/europe/*.

Contact: For more information on regional promotions, contact your local U.S. Export Assistance Center (USEAC). For the address and phone number of the USEAC nearest you, see Appendix A.

International Buyer Program, CS, ITA, U.S. Department of Commerce

The International Buyer Program of the U.S. Commercial Service brings thousands of qualified international buyers and prospective distributors and trade partners to the United States each year to meet with U.S. companies at approximately 35 major trade-only exhibitions. Without having to leave the country, U.S. exhibitors obtain worldwide promotion of their products and services and networking and matchmaking programs by country and industry experts.

Contact: For more information about the program, call Blanche Ziv, Global Trade Programs, at (202) 482-4207; fax (202) 482-0872; or e-mail *blanche.ziv@mail.doc.gov*. Information is also available at *www.export.gov.*

Overseas Trade Fair Certification, CS, ITA, U.S. Department of Commerce

The U.S. Department of Commerce's Trade Fair Certification Program is a cooperative partnership arrangement between private-sector show organizers and the U.S. government to increase U.S. exports and to expand U.S. participation in overseas trade shows. Through the CS, the program provides U.S. Department of Commerce endorsement, show-related services, oversight and coordination of event services, promotional support, exhibitor marketing facilitation, and in-country show site assistance for private-sector organizers to recruit and build a U.S. Pavilion at selected foreign trade shows. These shows serve a vital role in helping U.S. firms to enter and expand in foreign markets. The program ensures a high-quality, multifaceted opportunity for American companies to successfully market overseas.

Contact: For information on the Trade Fair Certification Program, write to Mike Thompson, manager, Trade Fair Certification, U.S. Department of Commerce, 1300 Pennsylvania Ave., Ronald Reagan Center, Suite 800M–Mezzanine Level–Atrium North, Washington, DC, 20004; call (202) 482-0671 or e-mail *michael.thompson@mail.doc.gov.*

Trade Fairs and Exhibitions, CS, ITA, U.S. Department of Commerce

In addition to certified shows, foreign and U.S. organizers hold many other good industry fairs of interest to U.S. exporters. CS staff members at U.S. embassies can identify these shows; arrange for participation; assist U.S. firms with market information; recommend pre- and post-event logistical and transportation support; and help exhibitors and visitors locate agents, distributors, and other potential buyers. Participation fees depend on the country and the show.

Contact: For information on trade show activities and a list of all types of trade events, call CS at 800-USA-TRAD(E) (800-872-8723), or view the trade events calendar online at *www. export.gov/tradeevents.*

Trade Missions, ITA, U.S. Department of Commerce

INTERNATIONAL TRADE ADMINISTRATION

Trade missions are an essential element of a broad-based public program designed to increase job opportunities for all Americans. The U.S. Department of Commerce offers several types of trade missions:

- *Commercial missions.* These missions seek to produce near-term export sales of U.S. goods and services from participating firms that travel as a group to one or more foreign markets. Appointments are made with officials and prospective business partners and customers. Commercial missions are organized for individual sectors or multiple industries and may include a range of companies. Some missions are planned specifically for small and medium-sized firms or minority- and women-owned businesses.

- *Market access missions.* These missions seek to create commercial opportunities through the removal of trade barriers and opening of markets for U.S. businesses that have been closed out of such opportunities.

- *Policy missions.* These missions seek to advance U.S. bilateral or multilateral objectives across a range of issues, with the objective of enhancing overall bilateral or multilateral economic and political relations. This category includes missions designed to promote political stability in a foreign country or region by fostering U.S. investment and trade.

- *Combined missions.* These missions embody aspects of two or more of the three previous missions.

- *Certified trade missions.* These missions are organized by state and private-sector trade promotion groups and are supported by the U.S. Department of Commerce. States, industry associations, and other groups should apply directly to a U.S. Department of Commerce overseas post to have their mission certified.

Contact: To find information on all missions, visit the trade events calendar at *www.export. gov/tradeevents*.

Product Literature Centers, Sample Displays, and International Catalog Exhibition Program, CS, ITA, U.S. Department of Commerce

The U.S. Commercial Service organizes Product Literature Centers and Sample Displays at international trade shows to spotlight U.S. exports. These industry-focused exhibits are attended by knowledgeable U.S. Department of Commerce industry or trade specialists or U.S. embassy officials who offer U.S. company literature and samples to hundreds of interested business prospects. Sales leads are sent directly to participating companies.

Contact: For more information on Product Literature Centers and Sample Displays, call 800-USA-TRAD(E) (800-872-8723), or visit *www.export.gov/tradeevents* (search by event type: International Catalog Exhibitions).

CHAPTER 6
SPECIAL MARKET ACCESS AND TECHNICAL ASSISTANCE

Advocacy Center, U.S. Commercial Service, International Trade Administration, U.S. Department of Commerce

The Advocacy Center is part of the U.S. Commercial Service (CS) of the International Trade Administration (ITA). The center coordinates U.S. government resources and authority in order to level the playing field on behalf of U.S. companies competing for specific international government projects and procurements. Because exporting today involves engaging foreign governments—not just offering a product or service at a competitive price—the Advocacy Center helps to ensure that U.S. products and services have the best possible chance to compete abroad. In situations where bidding processes for contracts are not open and transparent or are tilted in favor of non-U.S. competitors, the Advocacy Center develops and coordinates the actions of 19 U.S. government agencies on behalf of U.S. companies. The Advocacy Center works with businesses of every size to develop targeted business strategies and craft appropriate advocacy messages for delivery to foreign government decision-makers.

Contact: For more information, call the Advocacy Center at (202) 482-3896, fax (202) 482-3508, or visit *www.export.gov/advocacy.* You can also call the Trade Information Center at 800-USA-TRAD(E) (800-872-8723).

Multilateral Development Bank Commercial Liaisons, Advocacy Center, CS, ITA, U.S. Department of Commerce

The Advocacy Center's multilateral development bank (MDB) commercial liaison officers counsel U.S. firms about bidding opportunities for projects and procurements funded by the World Bank, the Asian Development Bank, the African Development Bank, the Inter-American Development Bank, and the European Bank for Reconstruction and Development. The liaison officers help U.S. companies to identify project and procurement information, troubleshoot procurement and contracting issues, advocate for fair consideration, and facilitate introductions to MDB decision-makers. These officers also organize outreach seminars and programs throughout the United States that are of interest to the U.S. private sector. The liaison officers facilitate investment strategies by introducing U.S. project sponsors or viable projects to the private-sector financing programs of the MDBs to finance social and economic infrastructure and privatization projects in developing countries.

Contacts: The banks may be contacted as follows: World Bank, Commercial Liaison Office: call (202) 458-0120, or fax (202) 477-2967; Inter-American Development Bank, Commercial Liaison Office: call (202) 623-3821, or fax (202) 623-2039; African Development Bank, Commercial Liaison Office (Tunisia): call +216.21.831.117, or fax +216.71.830.244; Asian Development Bank, Commercial Liaison Office (Philippines): call +632 887-1345, or fax +632 887-1164; and European Bank for Reconstruction and Development (United Kingdom): call +44 20 7588 8490, or fax +44 20 7588 8443. You can also call the Trade Information Center at 800-USA-TRAD(E) (800-872-8723).

Market Access and Compliance, ITA, U.S. Department of Commerce

The Market Access and Compliance (MAC) unit acts to open foreign markets for American goods and services by working with U.S. exporters to overcome foreign trade barriers and develop strategies to level the playing field. MAC specialists maintain in-depth knowledge of the trade policies and practices of U.S. trading partners. Working hand-in-hand with U.S. businesses, trade associations, and other U.S. government offices, MAC country, regional, and agreement experts develop information needed to conduct trade negotiations, monitor foreign country compliance with trade agreements, and ensure that U.S. firms know how to use market-opening agreements.

Contact: For appropriate contacts in MAC offices, call 800-USA-TRAD(E) (800-872-8723), or visit the MAC home page at *trade.gov/mac*.

CHAPTER 4
TRADE LEADS AND MARKET RESEARCH PROGRAMS

CUSTOMIZED PROGRAMS

International Partner Search, U.S. Commercial Service, International Trade Administration, U.S. Department of Commerce

The International Partner Search (IPS), a service of the U.S. Commercial Service (CS) of the International Trade Administration (ITA), helps U.S. companies find qualified international buyers, partners, or agents without traveling overseas. CS trade specialists will deliver detailed company information on up to five prescreened international companies that have expressed an interest in the U.S. firm's products and services. Fees depend on the scope of work.

Contact: For more information on IPS, contact the CS trade specialist at your local U.S. Export Assistance Center (USEAC). For the address and phone number of the USEAC nearest you, see Appendix A.

Gold Key Service, CS, ITA, U.S. Department of Commerce

The Gold Key Service, a program of the U.S. Commercial Service, helps U.S. companies secure one-on-one appointments with prescreened potential agents, distributors, sales representatives, association and government contacts, licensing or joint venture partners, and other strategic business partners in their targeted export markets. Fees depend on the scope of work.

Contact: For more information on the Gold Key Service, contact the CS trade specialist at your local USEAC. For the address and phone number of the USEAC nearest you, see Appendix A.

INTERNATIONAL
T R A D E
ADMINISTRATION

Trade Compliance Center, ITA, U.S. Department of Commerce

The Trade Compliance Center (TCC) administers ITA's Trade Agreements Compliance Program, through which the department systematically monitors, investigates, and ensures that foreign governments are in compliance with the international trade agreements to which the United States is party. The TCC serves as a one-stop shop for U.S. businesses that have encountered foreign trade barriers. Using the program's team approach, engaging all relevant Department of Commerce units, the TCC makes it unnecessary for U.S. companies to shop around the government for assistance. ITA teams strategize with U.S. businesses to reduce or eliminate such barriers and to assist them in gaining market access abroad.

The TCC maintains a comprehensive, free, and searchable Internet database of trade agreements and a Web site that assists both new and experienced exporters in understanding their rights and trading partners' obligations, as found in more than 270 bilateral and multilateral agreements covering trade in manufactured goods and services, including World Trade Organization (WTO) agreements, U.S. free trade agreements, and bilateral investment treaties.

The Web site also provides direct access to the TCC through its trade complaint "Hotline." Sending an e-mail through the Hotline to the TCC connects you to U.S. government trade policy assistance in resolving difficulties related to market access and trade agreements.

Contact: To contact the Trade Compliance Center, call (202) 482-1191, fax (202) 482-6097, or visit *www.trade.gov/tcc.* To report a trade barrier, visit *tcc.export.gov/report_a_barrier/.*

Strategy Targeting Organized Piracy, ITA, U.S. Department of Commerce

Growing global trade in pirated and counterfeit goods threatens the innovation economy of the United States, the competitiveness of leading U.S. companies and small manufacturers, and the livelihoods of their workers. The Strategy Targeting Organized Piracy (STOP!) initiative helps combat this problem by smashing criminal networks that traffic in counterfeit and pirated goods, stopping trade in these goods at U.S. borders, blocking these goods around the world, and helping small businesses secure and enforce their rights overseas.

As part of the STOP! initiative, a hotline has been established that provides one-stop shopping for businesses to protect their intellectual property at home and abroad. The STOP! hotline gives businesses the information they need to leverage the resources of the U.S. government to lock down and enforce their trademarks, patents, and copyrights overseas, both in individual countries and in multiple countries through international treaties.

Contact: For more information, or if you have concerns, call the hotline at 866-999-HALT (866-999-4258) or check the Web site at *www.stopfakes.gov.*

Antidumping/Countervailing Duty Petition Counseling and Analysis Unit, Import Administration, ITA, U.S. Department of Commerce

The Import Administration's Antidumping (AD)/Countervailing Duty (CVD) Petition Counseling and Analysis Unit has a dedicated staff of professionals who can offer guidance to U.S. companies regarding the provisions of U.S. unfair trade laws. Their vast experience extends to all aspects of antidumping and countervailing duty investigations, including

- Helping U.S. businesses understand U.S. unfair trade laws dealing with dumping and unfair foreign government subsidies
- Assisting U.S. companies that want to file petitions requesting the initiation of an investigation
- Helping potential petitioners to determine the types of information that will be required to pursue action against an industry suspected of unfair trade practices
- Assisting potential petitioners in ensuring that their petition complies with statutory initiation standards
- Providing small businesses with publicly available tariff and trade data from the U.S. Department of Commerce, the U.S. Department of the Treasury, and the U.S. International Trade Commission

Contact: For further information and assistance from a petition counselor, call the AD/CVD Petition Information Resource Center at (202) 482-1255, or e-mail *Petition_Counseling@ita.doc.gov.* For a prerecorded message of the most recent petitions filed, call the Petition Hotline at (202) 482-0430. Visit the AD/CVD Petition Counseling and Analysis Unit's Web site at *http://ia.ita.doc.gov/pcp/pcp-index.html.*

Export Trade Certificate of Review Program, ITA, U.S. Department of Commerce

Under the Export Trade Certificate of Review Program, U.S. firms can team up to gain economies of scale and share export costs and risks. The Certificate of Review offers antitrust preclearance on virtually any export activity, including joint negotiation with providers of export services regarding issues such as reduced shipping rates, agreements to sell together in export markets, agreements to form coalitions to avoid rivalry in export markets, coordination of export prices such as joint pricing, joint bidding on projects, and cost sharing on developing or expanding new export markets. This program provides firms with virtual immunity from antitrust liability at state and federal levels and significantly reduces their antitrust exposure at the private level.

Contact: To learn more about the program, call Export Trading Company Affairs at (202) 482-5131, or visit *www.ita.doc.gov/oetca.* To locate prospective U.S. export partners and export service firms, visit *www.myexports.com.*

ATA Carnet, U.S. Customs and Border Protection, U.S. Department of Homeland Security

The ATA Carnet is a special international customs document that may be used for temporary imports and exports—particularly professional equipment and commercial samples that are sent out of the country for less than one year. The ATA Carnet is issued in lieu of the usual customs documents and eliminates value added taxes, duties, and temporary import bonds. Seventy-five participating countries or territories accept the ATA Carnet as a guarantee against the payment of customs duties.

Contact: To contact the issuing authority, write to the United States Council for International Business, ATA Carnet Department, 1212 Avenue of the Americas, New York, NY 10036; call (866) 786-5625 or (212) 703-5078; fax (212) 944-0012; e-mail *atacarnet@uscib.org*; or visit *www.uscib.org*. For additional information, write to the U.S. Customs and Border Protection, Office of Field Operations, 1300 Pennsylvania Ave., NW, Washington, DC 20229; call (202) 344-1620; or visit *www.cbp.gov*.

Office of the United States Trade Representative

Staff members at the Office of the United States Trade Representative (USTR) can provide information to exporters confronted with problems involving the implementation of international trade agreements. Offices are organized according to sectoral, functional, and geographic responsibilities.

Contact: For more information, contact the following USTR personnel by phone: James Murphy, Agricultural Affairs, (202) 395-6127; Florizelle Liser, Office of Industry, (202) 395-5656; Joseph Papovich, Services, Investment, and Intellectual Property Rights, (202) 395-4510; David Spooner, Office of Textiles, (202) 395-3026; and Daniel Brinza, Monitoring and Enforcement, (202) 395-3582. The fax for all offices is (202) 395-3911. The USTR home page is *www.ustr.gov*.

Section 301 Relief, Office of the General Counsel, Office of the United States Trade Representative

The USTR is responsible for administering trade cases that provide relief from unfair trade practices under section 301 of the Trade Act of 1974. Individual exporters should contact the USTR concerning procedures for filing a complaint and defending U.S. interests and rights through the dispute settlement procedures of the WTO.

Contact: For section 301 assistance, call Daniel Brinza, assistant U.S. trade representative for monitoring and enforcement, at (202) 395-3582, or call William Busis, chairman, Section 301 Committee, at (202) 395-3150. You can also fax (202) 395-3639.

National Center for Standards and Certification Information, National Institute of Standards and Technology, U.S. Department of Commerce

The National Center for Standards and Certification Information (NCSCI) of the National Institute of Standards and Technology (NIST) provides electronic resources on U.S. and foreign standards and standards-related information, technical regulations, and conformity assessment requirements. The NCSCI provides the "Notify U.S." electronic service to inform interested parties (through e-mail notifications and customized Web sites) of new regulations or changes to existing regulations for 41 specific industry sectors in all WTO member countries. The NCSCI also assists U.S. exporters in identifying standards and directives for products to be marketed internationally. The center is the U.S. Inquiry Point for the WTO's Agreement on Technical Barriers to Trade, for the North American Free Trade Agreement, and for the International Organization for Standardization Information Network. The NCSCI is also the U.S. national standards information center.

Contact: For more information about the NCSCI, call (301) 975-4040, fax (301) 926-1559, e-mail *ncsci@nist.gov,* or visit *www.nist.gov/ncsci/.* Registration for "Notify U.S." can be done online at *www.nist.gov/notifyus/.*

Manufacturing Extension Partnership, NIST, U.S. Department of Commerce

NIST's Manufacturing Extension Partnership (MEP) is a national network with hundreds of specialists who understand the needs of manufacturers. For the past 20 years, they have worked with thousands of manufacturers, delivering $1.3 billion in cost savings annually.

MEP provides companies with services and access to public and private resources that enhance growth, improve productivity, and expand capacity. MEP specialists work with companies willing to invest in their future, to make improvements in the short term, and to position themselves to be stronger long-term competitors, both domestically and internationally.

Contact: For more information about MEP, access the NIST Web site at *www.mep.nist.gov,* call (301) 975-5020, or fax (301) 963-6556.

CE Mark Information for U.S. Manufacturers, NIST, U.S. Department of Commerce

NIST has published a pamphlet titled "To U.S. Manufacturers: Alert—Product 'Mark' Required for U.S. Exports to Europe." The pamphlet describes the steps involved in obtaining a CE mark, the mark required to sell many products in the European Union. The pamphlet includes a table showing conformity assessment procedures, a flowchart illustrating the European Declaration of Conformity, and a list of information resources so that U.S. manufacturers will know where to get copies of the applicable directives and where to obtain a list of standards.

Contact: To obtain a free copy of the pamphlet, call NIST at (301) 975-4040, or email *ncsci@ nist.gov*. The pamphlet is also available over the Internet at *www.export.gov/wcm/groups/ exportgov/documents/web_content/ce_mark_brochure.pdf.*

Laws and Metric Group, NIST, U.S. Department of Commerce

NIST's Laws and Metric Group provides guidance related to packaging and labeling requirements, net content requirements, and use of the metric system of measurement with the goal of making U.S. packaged goods more competitive in the export market and eliminating technical barriers to trade. The group also furnishes sources of information on metric standards and requirements in export markets.

Contact: To learn more about the group, call Elizabeth Gentry, group leader, at (301) 975-3690; fax (301) 975-8091; e-mail *TheSI@nist.gov*, or visit *www.nist.gov/metric.*

Bureau of Economic, Energy, and Business Affairs, U.S. Department of State

The Bureau of Economic, Energy, and Business Affairs integrates high-level economic expertise in areas such as international trade and investment policy, finance, telecommunications and information technology, energy and sanctions, international transportation issues, agriculture, and intellectual property rights with up-to-date information about economic and other developments around the world to advance U.S. interests.

The Office of Commercial and Business Affairs, which is part of the Bureau of Economic, Energy, and Business Affairs, works directly with the U.S. business community to help American companies tap into the worldwide resources of the U.S. Department of State. The office also champions U.S. business interests overseas with outreach, advocacy, investment climate information, and market access support. Under the April 20, 2008, memorandum of understanding with the U.S. Commercial Service, it leads State Department efforts to enhance delivery of commercial services and products in more than 100 countries that do not have U.S. Department of Commerce operations. The office also engages business leaders on a variety of competitiveness issues that affect them (such as business travel, visas, and export controls licenses).

Contact: For more information, call the Office of Commercial and Business Affairs at (202) 647-1625, fax (202) 647-3953, or visit *www.state.gov/travelandbusiness.*

Bureau of Consular Affairs, U.S. Department of State

The U.S. Department of State's Bureau of Consular Affairs recognizes that business travel to the United States by foreign employees, customers, and potential clients of U.S. firms is critical to the success of U.S. businesses. Realizing that a vibrant business relationship with all nations contributes to progress toward a more secure and prosperous world, the State Department has developed several initiatives to assist international business travelers. For instance, in January 2006, the secretary of state and the secretary of homeland security announced the Rice–Chertoff Joint Vision Initiative, which is designed to facilitate the visa process for the foreign employees, partners, and customers of U.S. businesses. Building on the use of the electronic nonimmigrant visa application, the State Department is currently piloting a paperless visa system, just one of several measures that will allow business and other travelers to enter the United States more efficiently. The State Department works with countries to increase visa reciprocity, which allows travelers to receive visas that are valid for a longer period of time.

All U.S. embassies and consulates have established procedures to expedite the processing of business visas. U.S. officials also work closely with American chambers of commerce in more than 100 countries to expedite the visa process for legitimate business travelers.

The U.S. Department of State's Business Visa Center in Washington, D.C., facilitates visa application procedures for U.S. companies and convention organizers who invite employees or current and prospective business clients to the United States. The center handled more than 5,000 requests from American businesses for information and assistance in cases involving more than 311,000 business travelers in fiscal year 2007.

Contact: For more information on visas and appointments, visit *www.travel.state.gov*. To contact the Business Visa Center, call (202) 663-3198, or e-mail *BusinessVisa@state.gov*.

Workshops and Conferences, U.S. Trade and Development Agency

The U.S. Trade and Development Agency (USTDA) organizes workshops, conferences, and technical symposia worldwide. These events are sector or project oriented and are aimed at connecting overseas project sponsors with U.S. firms and entities that supply project finance, technology, and industry expertise that may be useful in project implementation. USTDA contracts with prequalified professional conference specialists to organize these activities.

Contact: For more information, call the USTDA Information Resource Center at (703) 875-4357, fax (703) 875-4009, e-mail *info@ustda.gov*, or visit *www.ustda.gov*.

CHAPTER 7
EXPORT FINANCE, INSURANCE, AND GRANTS (NON-AGRICULTURAL)

EXPORT FINANCE

Trade Finance Guide, International Trade Administration, U.S. Department of Commerce

INTERNATIONAL
TRADE
ADMINISTRATION

In 2007, the Office of Finance of the International Trade Administration (ITA) issued the first edition of the *Trade Finance Guide: A Quick Reference for U.S. Exporters*. With the guide in high demand by the exporting community, a second edition was published in April 2008. The guide is targeted to small and medium-sized enterprises, with concise, two-page chapters that offer the basics of numerous financing techniques and the specific situations for considering each. The latest edition includes a chapter on foreign exchange risk management as well as updates to all of the other chapters. The guide was created in partnership with the Association of Executives in Finance, Credit, and International Business (FCIB) and with the cooperation of the U.S. Small Business Administration (SBA), the Export–Import Bank, and various other private trade associations. For a printed copy, call the Trade Information Center at 800-USA-TRAD(E) (800-872-8723) or U.S. Export Assistance Centers (USEACs) nationwide. For the PDF format, visit *www.ita.doc.gov/media/Publications/abstract/trade_finance_guide2008desc.html*.

Export–Import Bank of the United States

The Export–Import (Ex–Im) Bank provides a variety of export finance assistance, including export credit insurance, preexport financing through working capital guaranteed loans to exporters, and medium- and long-term loans and guarantees to overseas buyers. Ex–Im Bank offers various programs to the business community, including regular seminars and group briefings at several locations around the country. Specific Ex–Im Bank programs are described in this chapter.

Contact: For information on all Ex–Im Bank programs, call the export financing hotline at (800) 565-3946. Select option 2 to automatically switch the call to the nearest regional office. The Ex–Im Bank home page is *www.exim.gov*.

City–State Program, Ex–Im Bank of the United States

Ex–Im Bank works with state, county, and local non-profit economic development entities to offer marketing support to them and financial assistance to exporters in their jurisdictions. Cooperative programs currently operate in more than 50 states and regions, as well as in Puerto Rico.

Contact: To learn more about the City–State Program, call Gus Grace, business development officer, at (202) 565-3910; fax (202) 565-3930; or e-mail *gus.grace@exim.gov*.

Regional Offices, Ex–Im Bank of the United States

Ex–Im Bank's regional offices provide services and information to businesses. Regional offices are in Orange County, California; San Diego, California; San Francisco, California; Miami, Florida; Chicago, Illinois; New York, New York; Dallas, Texas; Houston, Texas; and Washington, D.C. Ex–Im Bank is also represented at most USEACs.

Contact: The regional offices are as follows: Orange County, California: call (949) 660-1341, or fax (949) 660-9553; San Diego, California: call (619) 557-7091, or fax (619) 557-6176; San Francisco, California: call (415) 705-2285, or fax (415) 705-1156; Miami, Florida: call (305) 526-7436, or fax (305) 526-7435; Chicago, Illinois: call (312) 353-8081, or fax (312) 353-8098; New York, New York: call (212) 809-2650, or fax (212) 809-2687; Dallas, Texas: call (214) 551-4959, or fax (214) 377-4185; Houston, Texas: call (281) 721-0465, or fax (281) 679-0156; Washington, D.C.: call (202) 565-3946, or fax (202) 565-3932. For the addresses and phone numbers of USEACs, see Appendix A.

Working Capital Guarantee Program, Ex–Im Bank of the United States

The Working Capital Guarantee Program helps small and medium-sized businesses obtain critical preexport financing from commercial lenders. Ex–Im Bank guarantees 90 percent of the principal and interest on transaction-specific loans or revolving lines of credit that are extended to eligible exporters. The funds may be used for preexport activities, which include the purchase of raw materials, labor, overhead, performance bonds, retainers, and warranties.

Contact: For more information about the Working Capital Guarantee Program, call Pamela Bowers at (202) 565-3792, fax (202) 565-3793, visit *www.exim.gov*, or contact an Ex–Im Bank regional office.

Export Credit Insurance, Ex–Im Bank of the United States

Ex–Im Bank offers insurance policies that cover political and commercial risks on export receivables:

- **Small business policy.** This policy is available to firms just beginning to export or with average annual export credit sales of less than $5 million for the past two years. These businesses must also meet the SBA definition of a *small business*. The policy offers enhanced coverage, a lower premium than usually found in other insurance policies, and an enhanced assignment used to discount receivables with a bank. Special features are also available for exporters of environmental goods and services.
- **Bank letter of credit policy.** This policy insures commercial banks against loss on irrevocable letters of credit issued by foreign banks on behalf of importers purchasing U.S. goods and services.
- **Multibuyer policy.** This policy insures all of an exporter's short-term export credit sales or a reasonable spread of risk.
- **Financial institution buyer credit policy.** This policy insures individual short-term export credits extended by financial institutions to foreign buyers.
- **Short-term single-buyer policy.** This policy allows exporters to insure receivables against losses attributable to commercial and specified political risks on a selective basis.

Contact: For more information, call Ex–Im Bank's Business Development Office at (202) 565-3900, fax (202) 565-3932, visit *www.exim.gov*, or contact an Ex–Im Bank regional office.

Guarantees, Ex–Im Bank of the United States

This program extends three-to-seven-year term financing in the form of guarantees to creditworthy foreign buyers of U.S. capital goods or services. The loans and guarantees offered are for 85 percent of the U.S. export value. The guarantee coverage provides protection to the source of financing against payment default for political or commercial reasons. Interest rates for the guarantees are negotiated between the source of financing and the seller and are typically floating rates. Political-only guarantee coverage is also available. In addition, Ex–Im Bank is willing to provide support for a broad range of environmental exports, including special transaction structures for certain lease transactions, industrial design services, architectural or engineering services, and overseas operations and maintenance contracts.

Contact: To learn more, call Ex–Im Bank's Business Development Office at (202) 565-3900, fax (202) 565-3932, visit *www.exim.gov*, or contact an Ex–Im Bank regional office.

Limited Recourse Project Finance Program, Ex–Im Bank of the United States

The Limited Recourse Project Finance Program provides financing for projects that depend on the cash flows of the project for repayment and not on recourse to a foreign government, a financial institution, or an established corporation. Combinations of direct loans, political risk–only coverage, or comprehensive guarantees for commercial bank loans are available. Ex–Im Bank now offers precompletion comprehensive coverage for selected projects. Ex–Im Bank offerings include financing of up to 85 percent of the U.S. export value, financing of interest during construction, and financing of local costs in the host country of up to 30 percent of the U.S. contract value and up to the maximum repayment terms consistent with the guidelines of the Organization for Economic Cooperation and Development.

Contact: For more information on the program, call Kristine Wood at (202) 565-3913, fax (202) 565-3695, or visit *www.exim.gov.*

U.S. Small Business Administration

The SBA offers several loan programs that help small and medium-sized enterprises start or expand their small business operations in amounts ranging from $5,000 to $4 million. The SBA sets the guidelines for the loans while its partners (banks, community development organizations, and microlending institutions) make the actual loans. The SBA backs the loans with a guarantee that will eliminate some of the risk to the lending partners.

Contact: The Web site for SBA loan programs is *www.sba.gov/financing.*

Business Loan Guarantee Program, Small Business Administration

The SBA's 7(a) program helps qualified small businesses obtain financial assistance from banks. The SBA can guarantee 7(a) loans to businesses engaged in manufacturing, construction, wholesale, retail, or service industries. The proceeds may be used to acquire equipment, facilities, machinery, supplies, or materials; to obtain working capital; to finance construction, conversion, or expansion; and to refinance existing debt.

The maximum loan size is $2.0 million. The maximum dollar amount that SBA will guarantee is $1.5 million. The maximum maturity is 25 years. The maturity is based on the useful life of the assets being financed. For loans that provide working capital, the maturity can be up to 7 years; for equipment loans, up to 10 years; and for real estate loans, up to 25 years. Interest rates on SBA guarantee loans are negotiated between the applicant and the lender and may not exceed SBA maximums.

Contact: For the nearest SBA district office or USEAC, call 800-U-ASK-SBA (800-827-5722), or visit *www.sba.gov/financing.*

SBA Export Finance, Small Business Administration

SBA Export Finance programs for small business exporters take the form of loan guarantees to participating lenders who provide the capital. Three different programs are offered:

- **Export Working Capital Program.** The Export Working Capital Program (EWCP) provides transaction financing for small exporters. The loans can be structured to support financing for single transactions, export contracts, and lines of credit. The loan term is typically one year or less. Preshipment financing can cover materials, labor, and export-related costs; postshipment financing of the export receivables and standby letters of credit used as performance bonds; and payment guarantee or bid bonds. With the co-guarantee agreement between the SBA and Ex-Im Bank, EWCP loans can be approved for up to $2 million using a single application. Interest rates and fees are negotiated between business and lender. The SBA guarantee fee is one-quarter of 1 percent for EWCPs with a maturity of 12 months or fewer. Application information is available from USEACs.

- **International Trade Loan Program.** International trade loans can be used to finance equipment and facilities and to refinance loans originally used for these purposes. Companies that are new to export, exporters needing to expand, or companies adversely affected by import competition are eligible to apply. Loan maturity can be up to 25 years. Application is made through SBA lenders. Interest rates and fees are negotiated between business and lender.

- **Export Express Program.** Export Express loans can finance a variety of export-related costs: market development (for trade shows, translation of product literature, and so forth); transaction costs; equipment for the production of goods to be exported; and standby letters of credit for bid and performance bonds or payment guarantees. The maximum loan amount is $250,000. Application for this loan is through SBA Express lenders, who are able to use their own forms, documentation, and approval process. The SBA provides approvals within 24 hours or less. To be eligible, small businesses must have been in business for one year and must plan to export. Interest rates and fees are negotiated between business and lender.

Contact: For more information on these programs, visit *www.sba.gov/international*, or contact the SBA staff in the USEACs. In September 2008, the SBA's Office of International Trade released the 4th edition of *Breaking into the Trade Game: A Small Business Guide to Exporting.* To access this guide on the basics of exporting, visit the Office of International Trade's Web site at *www.sba.gov/international*.

Small Business Investment Companies, Small Business Administration

Small business investment companies (SBICs), licensed by the SBA, are privately owned and managed venture capital and investment firms. Although SBICs are licensed, are regulated, and may receive supplemental funding through SBA guarantees, all investment decisions are made by SBICs. SBICs are required to invest domestically; however, they may invest in businesses that have an export focus.

Contact: To learn more about SBICs, call the SBA's Investment Division at (202) 205-6510, or visit *www.sba.gov/inv.*

Untied Aid Initiatives, ITA, U.S. Department of Commerce

Untied aid is financing provided by wealthier countries to developing countries and emerging markets for development projects. It is primarily provided in the form of concessional loans, where procurement is not contingent on the purchase of goods and services from the donor country. Untied aid can offer U.S. firms significant business opportunities.

U.S. firms interested in pursuing procurement opportunities associated with untied aid–funded projects should familiarize themselves with the Organization for Economic Cooperation and Development (OECD), which provides information on projects financed with bilateral untied aid on two of its Web sites:

* The first Web site is maintained by the OECD's Export Credit Secretariat and is based on a U.S. proposal to open the bidding process for projects in developing countries that are financed with untied aid credits. The agreement sets multilateral requirements for OECD governments to report publicly on the details of their untied aid–financed projects, including the outcome of each bid competition. For information on these projects, visit *http://webdomino1.oecd.org/COMNET/ECH/xuntied.nsf?Opendatabase.*

* The second Web site is the untied aid bulletin board of the OECD's Development Assistance Committee, *www.oecd.org/dac/untiedaid.* It is based on a 2001 agreement to provide untied aid notifications for projects in the least developed countries.

Contact: For more information on untied aid initiatives, contact ITA: call Danius Barzdukas, Office of Japan, at (202) 482-1147; fax (202) 482-0469; or e-mail *danius_barzdukas@ita.doc. gov;* or call Denise Carpenter, Office of Finance, at (202) 482-4002; fax (202) 482-5702; or e-mail *denise_carpenter@ita.doc.gov.* You can also visit ITA's Office of Finance Web site at *www.ita.doc.gov/td/finance/2.html.*

OVERSEAS INVESTMENT FINANCE

Overseas Private Investment Corporation

The Overseas Private Investment Corporation (OPIC) helps U.S. businesses invest overseas, fosters economic development in new and emerging markets, complements the private sector in managing risks associated with foreign direct investment, and supports U.S. foreign policy. Because OPIC charges market-based fees for its products, it operates on a self-sustaining basis at no net cost to taxpayers. OPIC promotes U.S. best practices by requiring that projects adhere to international standards on the environment, workers' rights, and human rights.

Contact: To learn more, call the OPIC InfoLine at (202) 336-8799, fax (202) 408-9859, or visit *www.opic.gov.* Callers with a touchtone phone may listen to brief recorded program descriptions and request that printed program information be sent to them by way of mail or fax, or any callers may—from 8:45 a.m. to 5:30 p.m. EST—speak with an OPIC information officer.

Investment Insurance, Overseas Private Investment Corporation

OPIC offers several programs to insure U.S. investments in emerging markets and developing countries against the risks of (a) currency inconvertibility (the inability to convert profits, debt service, and other investment remittances from local currency into U.S. dollars or the inability to transfer funds); (b) expropriation (loss of an investment because of expropriation, nationalization, or confiscation by the host government); and (c) political violence (loss of assets or income because of war, revolution, insurrection, or politically motivated civil strife, terrorism, or sabotage). Coverage is available for new ventures, expansion of existing enterprises, privatizations, and acquisitions with positive developmental benefits. Coverage is also available for equity investments, parent company and third-party loans and loan guarantees, technical assistance agreements, leases, consigned inventory or equipment, and other forms of investment.

Contact: For more information, call the OPIC InfoLine at (202) 336-8799, fax (202) 408-9859, or visit *www.opic.gov.*

Finance Programs, Overseas Private Investment Corporation

OPIC provides financing through direct loans and loan guarantees for medium- and long-term private investment. Loans range from $100,000 to $250 million for projects sponsored by U.S. companies, and financing can be provided on a project finance or corporate finance basis. In most cases, the U.S. sponsor is expected to contribute at least 25 percent of the project equity, have a track record in the industry, and have the means to contribute to the financial success of the project. For U.S. small businesses with annual revenues under $35 million, OPIC's Small Business Center can provide financing through a streamlined approval process and an "insurance wrap" that offers political risk insurance coverage at a reduced rate.

Additionally, to address the lack of sufficient equity investment in emerging markets, OPIC has supported the creation of privately owned and managed investment funds that make direct equity and equity-related investments in new, expanding, or privatizing companies.

Contact: To find out about finance programs, call the OPIC InfoLine at (202) 336-8799, fax (202) 408-9859, or visit *www.opic.gov*.

Enterprise Development Network, Overseas Private Investment Corporation

In June 2007, OPIC launched the Enterprise Development Network (EDN), a strategic alliance with the private sector that greatly expands OPIC's ability to provide financing and political risk insurance to U.S. micro, small, and medium-sized enterprises (MSMEs) doing business in developing countries. Through the support of financial institutions, business consultants, associations, law firms, and regional investment promotion agencies, EDN eases MSMEs' access to OPIC products and services. By empowering such private-sector service providers, the network delivers services to American businesses more efficiently and cost-effectively, thereby improving access to credit that is often difficult to obtain for overseas projects. It also unlocks an entirely new niche market for lenders and other service providers, offering them a valuable opportunity to expand their client bases into emerging markets overseas and a new means to service those clients by decreasing capital requirements for their financing.

Contact: For more information, call the OPIC InfoLine at (202) 336-8799, fax (202) 408-9859, or visit *www.opic.gov*.

GRANTS AND FUNDING FOR FEASIBILITY STUDIES AND OTHER EXPORT-RELATED NEEDS

Feasibility Studies, U.S. Trade and Development Agency

The U.S. Trade and Development Agency (USTDA) provides grants for overseas infrastructure project–planning assistance, such as feasibility studies. These studies evaluate the technical, financial, environmental, legal, and other critical aspects of infrastructure development projects that are of interest to potential lenders and investors. Project sponsors in the host countries select the U.S. companies that perform USTDA-funded feasibility studies. Normally, selection is made through open competitions.

Contact: For more information, call the USTDA Information Resource Center at (703) 875-4357, fax (703) 875-4009, or e-mail *info@ustda.gov*. A model proposal format can be found on USTDA's Web site at *www.ustda.gov*.

Technical Assistance Grants, U.S. Trade and Development Agency

USTDA provides technical assistance to help with the development of sector strategies, industry standards, and legal and regulatory regimes. This assistance helps create a favorable business and trade environment. Transportation safety and security are particularly important sectors for USTDA's technical assistance work.

Contact: To learn more about technical assistance grants, call the USTDA Information Resource Center at (703) 875-4357, fax (703) 875-4009, or e-mail *info@ustda.gov*. A model proposal format can be found on USTDA's Web site at *www.ustda.gov*.

Desk Studies and Definitional Missions, U.S. Trade and Development Agency

One of the earliest stages of project planning is the development of terms of reference for an activity that will define the technical, environmental, financial, and other factors that must be addressed before an investment decision can be made. USTDA helps ensure that a project is appropriately conceived by contracting with technical specialists to perform definitional missions and desk studies. These independent assessments develop the appropriate terms of reference and budget for pertinent project preparation activities. Using U.S. private-sector resources and expertise, these activities provide preliminary assessments of the economic viability of proposed projects and determine whether they meet USTDA's funding criteria.

Contact: Direct contracting opportunities with USTDA are posted on the Federal Business Opportunities Web site at *www.fedbizopps.gov.* Small businesses interested in providing USTDA with consultant services related to project evaluations should register with USTDA's On-Line Consultant Database at *www.ustda.gov* and with the federal government's Central Contractor Registration Web site at *www.ccr.gov.* Questions should be directed to USTDA's Information Resource Center: call (703) 875-4357, fax (703) 875-4009, or e-mail *info@ustda.gov.*

Training Grants, U.S. Trade and Development Agency

USTDA provides training for foreign decision-makers in economic sectors where there are opportunities for the sale of U.S. equipment and services. The training is normally focused on technology or regulatory issues and is designed to give project sponsors a better understanding of U.S. experience and capabilities. Training can be conducted in the United States or in the host country.

Contact: To learn more about training grants, call the USTDA Information Resource Center at (703) 875-4357, fax (703) 875-4009, e-mail *info@ustda.gov,* or visit *www.ustda.gov.*

INTERNATIONAL
TRADE
ADMINISTRATION

Market Development Cooperator Program Awards, ITA, U.S. Department of Commerce

The Market Development Cooperator Program (MDCP) is a competitive matching funds program operated by ITA. The program builds public–private partnerships by providing federal assistance to non-profit export multipliers such as states, trade associations, chambers of commerce, and small business development centers. These multipliers can be particularly effective in helping small and medium-sized enterprises to be more competitive. Applicants use their own creativity to design projects that will help such enterprises enter, expand, or maintain market share in targeted markets abroad. MDCP awards help underwrite the start-up costs of new foreign market–development ventures.

Contact: To learn more about the program, call the MDCP program manager at (202) 482-2969, or visit *www.export.gov/mdcp.*

Special American Business Internship Training, ITA, U.S. Department of Commerce

The Special American Business Internship Training (SABIT) Program is a public–private initiative to promote market access and to cultivate economic and civil society development in various countries in Eurasia: Armenia, Azerbaijan, Belarus, Georgia, Kazakhstan, Kyrgyzstan, Moldova, Russia, Tajikistan, Turkmenistan, Ukraine, and Uzbekistan. The SABIT Program provides industry-specific group training programs for Eurasian professionals. These training programs balance the technical assistance needs of Eurasia's emerging markets with the interests of the U.S. business community. Since 1990, the SABIT Program has enabled more than 2,500 U.S. organizations to host more than 4,000 trainees.

Contact: To learn more about the SABIT Program, call (202) 482-0073, fax (202) 482-2443, or visit *www.mac.doc.gov/sabit.*

CHAPTER 8
AGRICULTURAL EXPORT AND FINANCE PROGRAMS

AGRICULTURAL EXPORT PROGRAMS

Foreign Agricultural Service Web Site, U.S. Department of Agriculture

The Foreign Agricultural Service (FAS) Web site provides users with information about FAS's efforts to improve foreign market access for U.S. products, to build new markets, to improve the competitive position of U.S. agriculture in the global marketplace, and to provide food aid and technical assistance to foreign countries. The Web site provides users access to the export credit guarantee and food aid programs of the U.S. Department of Agriculture (USDA), as well as to updates on USDA efforts to increase income and food availability in developing nations by mobilizing expertise for agriculturally led economic growth.

Contact: Visit the FAS Web site at *www.fas.usda.gov*.

Export Marketing Services, FAS, U.S. Department of Agriculture

FAS offers the following export marketing services to assist new and experienced exporters in finding customers overseas:

- *Foreign Buyers List.* This list provides information on more than 25,000 foreign buyers of food, farm, fish, seafood, and forest products in more than 80 countries. The fee is $15 per list (by product for a specific country). For more information, visit *www.fas.usda.gov/agexport/forbuy.html*.

- *Export Directory of U.S. Food Distribution Companies.* This directory provides information on U.S. suppliers of mixed containers of grocery and food service products to foreign buyers. Registration is free of charge. For more information, visit *www.fas.usda.gov/AgExport/Directory/Main.html*.

- *U.S. Supplier List.* This searchable database provides data for more than 3,500 U.S. exporters and their products (more than 500 product categories) and is used by FAS to help connect potential buyers with U.S. suppliers. Registration is free of charge. For more information, visit *http://fas1.agexportservices.org/Apps/StoreFronts/search.asp*.

- **State Regional Trade Groups.** U.S. suppliers who want to inform foreign buyers about their products may contact the State Regional Trade Groups (SRTGs) for assistance. The SRTGs, which are FAS program participants, offer customized export assistance on a wide variety of export-related topics from "connection to collection." To obtain the SRTGs directory, visit *www.fas.usda.gov/agx/counseling_advocacy/srtg_directory.asp*.

Contact: Questions about any of these services should be directed to USDA's Foreign Agricultural Service at (202) 690-3576.

National Agricultural Library, U.S. Department of Agriculture

The National Agricultural Library (NAL) is a repository of information on agricultural marketing and trade. NAL staff members respond to inquiries with customized assistance by combining in-depth knowledge of the library's resources, state-of-the-art technology, and networking. They also assist users in accessing the library's online catalog and article citation database, AGRICOLA (Agricultural Online Access database).

Contact: To learn more, call the NAL Service Desk at (301) 504-5755, fax (301) 504-6110, or e-mail *agref@nal.usda.gov*. The NAL home page is *www.nal.usda.gov*, and the AGRICOLA home page is *http://agricola.nal.usda.gov*.

Economic Research Service, U.S. Department of Agriculture

The Economic Research Service (ERS) provides in-depth economic analyses on agricultural economies, trade policies of foreign countries, world agricultural trade and development issues, and their links with the U.S. food and fiber economy. ERS analyzes how factors influencing demand (population, income, and tastes); production variables (inputs and technology); foreign governments' commercial policies and programs (price controls, environmental and food safety laws, and tariffs); macroeconomic conditions (exchange rates and debt); and major events (for example, China's accession to the World Trade Organization) affect countries' agricultural production, consumption, and trade; international food and fiber prices; and U.S. food and fiber competitiveness. ERS widely disseminates information and analyses on international agricultural trade, food aid, and development through regional and commodity reports, bulletins and updates, periodicals, and electronic databases.

Contact: For more information, call Cheryl Christensen, deputy director, Market and Trade Economics Division, at (202) 694-5203; fax (202) 694-5792; or e-mail *cherylc@ers.usda.gov*. The ERS home page is *www.ers.usda.gov*.

Trade Shows, FAS, U.S. Department of Agriculture

The USDA Overseas Trade Support Branch offers U.S. food and beverage exporters a choice of programs to satisfy their marketing needs. Programs include endorsed shows in leading and emerging markets worldwide, as well as American Cafés. When USDA links its name with a show, you can be assured of high standards at a fair price. USDA will give companies marketing services, including reports on the country and its buyers, and even limited public relations help. In addition, the USDA Overseas Trade Support Branch provides information on the promoters of other international food and beverage shows.

Contact: For more information, call the USDA Overseas Trade Support Branch at (202) 690-1182, fax (202) 690-4374, or visit *www.fas.usda.gov/agx/trade_events/tsmo.asp*.

Business and Cooperative Programs, Rural Development, U.S. Department of Agriculture

USDA's Rural Development unit offers a number of business and cooperative programs that are intended to enhance the quality of life for rural Americans by providing leadership in building competitive businesses, including sustainable cooperatives that can prosper in the global marketplace. Business programs comprise a number of loan and grant programs, including the Business and Industry Guaranteed Loan Program, the Intermediary Relending Program, the Rural Business Enterprise Grant Program, and the Rural Business Opportunity Grant Program.

The Cooperative Services Program promotes the use of the cooperative form of business as a viable organizational option for marketing and distributing agricultural products. The program offers technical assistance to those wishing to form new cooperatives. Funding opportunities include Rural Cooperative Development Grants, Small Minority Producer Grants, and Value-Added Producer Grants. Among the other services provided are a directory of cooperatives, a map of state resources, and the monthly publication of *Rural Cooperative Magazine*.

Contact: For more information about the programs, visit *www.rurdev.usda.gov/rbs/*. Business and cooperative programs are administered by Rural Development field staff members. Field office information is available at *www.rurdev.usda.gov/recd_map.html*, or call (800) 670-6553.

AGRICULTURAL TECHNICAL ASSISTANCE

Agricultural Marketing Service, Transportation Services Division, U.S. Department of Agriculture

USDA's Agricultural Marketing Service administers programs that facilitate the efficient and fair marketing of U.S. agricultural products, including food, fiber, and specialty crops. Services offered include

- Regulatory representation
- Economic analysis
- Technical assistance
- Outreach
- Response to inquiries

Contact: To learn more, call (202) 690-1304, fax (202) 690-3616, or visit *www.ams.usda.gov/AMSv1.0/*.

Publications and Resources, Agricultural Marketing Service, Transportation Services Division, U.S. Department of Agriculture

Exporting is more than just locating a buyer and making the sale. Getting the product to your overseas customer in the best condition, on time, and at the most reasonable cost is also an integral part of the export process and can turn new customers into repeat customers. The Agricultural Marketing Service provides transportation market reports, logistics publications, and technical assistance for agricultural shippers navigating the complexities of the export process. In addition, it provides publications geared specifically to various agricultural subsectors.

Contact: For additional information, visit *www.ams.usda.gov/AMSv1.0/* and click on "Publications."

AGRICULTURAL FINANCE AND GRANT PROGRAMS

The Commodity Credit Corporation (CCC) administers two export credit guarantee programs for commercial financing of U.S. agricultural exports. The Export Credit Guarantee Program (GSM-102) encourages exports of U.S. agricultural commodities to buyers in countries where credit is necessary to maintain or increase U.S. sales but where commercial financing may not be available without CCC guarantees. The Facility Guarantee Program encourages exports of capital goods and services from the United States that improve transport, storage, and handling of U.S. exported agricultural commodities in emerging markets. In both programs, CCC undertakes a significant portion of foreign bank risk. Program announcements issued by USDA provide information on specific country and commodity allocations, length of credit period, coverage of shipping terms, approved countries and banks, and applicable risk-based fees to register the sales. Specific program details are as follows:

- The Export Credit Guarantee Program (GSM-102) guarantees payment by a foreign bank on credit extended by a financial institution in the United States (or, less commonly, by a U.S. exporter) to pay for food and agricultural commodities produced in the United States and sold to foreign buyers. The related obligations must be repaid in U.S. dollars. The program can cover credit terms ranging from 30 days to three years.

- The Facility Guarantee Program (FGP) provides payment guarantees to facilitate the financing of manufactured goods and services exported from the United States. FGP is designed to improve handling, marketing, processing, storage, and distribution of imported agricultural products in emerging markets where it is determined that the FGP payment guarantees will promote exports of U.S. agricultural products. FGP requires a down payment on the eligible contract value and covers a significant portion of the remaining principal balance and a portion of interest. There must, however, be a primary benefit to U.S. agricultural products sold overseas. There is no application fee.

Contact: To learn more about these programs, call the Registrations and Operations Branch of FAS at (202) 720-3224, e-mail *AskGSM@fas.usda.gov*, or visit *www.fas.usda.gov/ exportprograms.asp*.

Export Market Development Programs, FAS, U.S. Department of Agriculture

FAS offers the following export market development programs:

- The Market Access Program (MAP) uses funds from the USDA's Commodity Credit Corporation to provide cost-share assistance to U.S. trade organizations and small entities to help create, expand, and maintain foreign markets for U.S. agricultural commodities and products. MAP participants must contribute a minimum of 10 percent of the cost of generic marketing and promotion activities and 50 percent for branded promotions.

- The Foreign Market Development (FMD) Program, also known as the Cooperator Program, assists non-profit U.S. agricultural trade organizations in developing and maintaining foreign markets for U.S. agricultural products through a cost-share program. FMD funds are allocated to U.S. trade organizations with the broadest possible producer representation. Priority is given to organizations that are nationwide in membership and scope. Activities must contribute to the maintenance or growth of demand for agricultural commodities and generally address long-term foreign import constraints and export growth opportunities.

- The Emerging Markets Program (EMP) assists U.S. public and private organizations in improving market opportunities for U.S. agricultural products in low- to middle-income countries with market potential. The program can be used for technical assistance, such as activities that focus on building trade capacity or addressing technical barriers to trade. The EMP has a cost-sharing requirement.

- The Quality Samples Program provides funding to help U.S. organizations supply samples of U.S. commodities to potential foreign buyers and provide technical assistance regarding product quality and proper use as a means to encourage new purchases. The program supports projects that benefit whole industries rather than individual companies. When a project is finished, USDA reimburses the costs of procuring and exporting the samples.

- The Technical Assistance for Specialty Crops Program helps to open, retain, and expand markets for U.S. specialty crops. Resources are provided to address barriers, including phytosanitary or related technical restrictions that prohibit or threaten the export of U.S. specialty crops. Specialty crops include all cultivated plants and their products produced in the United States except wheat, feed grains, oilseeds, cotton, rice, peanuts, sugar, and tobacco.

Contact: For more information, call FAS at (202) 720-4327, or visit *www.fas.usda.gov/ exportprograms.asp.*

CHAPTER 9

HEALTH, PERFORMANCE, QUALITY, AND SAFETY INSPECTION AND
CERTIFICATION PROGRAMS

U.S.–European Union Safe Harbor Framework for Privacy, Data Protection, and
Cross Border Data Flows, International Trade Administration, U.S. Department of
Commerce

The Safe Harbor Framework is a voluntary, self-certification system that is designed to help
U.S. companies avoid interruptions in their business dealings with the European Union (EU)
or prosecution by European authorities under European privacy laws. The EU Directive
on Data Protection took effect in 1998 and prohibits the transfer of personally identifiable
information to non-EU nations that fail to meet the European "adequacy" standard for
privacy protection. As a result of the differing approaches to privacy established by the
European Commission and the United States, this EU directive can significantly hamper
the ability of U.S. companies to engage in many trans-Atlantic transactions, including
e-commerce. The Safe Harbor Framework was developed by the U.S. Department of
Commerce, in consultation with the EU, industry, and non-governmental organizations, to
bridge these different privacy approaches and to provide a streamlined means for U.S.
organizations to comply with the EU directive.

Contact: Certification may be submitted on the Internet or to Damon Greer, director, U.S.–EU
Safe Harbor Framework, Room 2003, International Trade Administration, Department of
Commerce, 1401 Constitution Avenue, NW, Washington, DC 20230; phone, (202) 482-5023;
fax, (202) 482-5522; or e-mail, *damon.greer@mail.doc.gov*. The Safe Harbor home page is
http://export.gov/safeharbor/.

Export Certificates for U.S. Products, Food and Drug Administration

Foreign customers and governments often request that U.S. companies submit an export certificate when they ship products regulated by the Food and Drug Administration (FDA) abroad. FDA export certificates are for export purposes only and may not be used in domestic advertising or promotion. The FDA, at the request of U.S. exporters, will issue export certificates for human drugs and biological products, animal drugs, and medical devices that meet the applicable requirements of the Federal Food, Drug, and Cosmetic Act. The FDA certifies that the products meet domestic U.S. requirements and are eligible for sale in the United States. In cases where the product may not be marketed in the United States, the FDA certifies that the product may be exported under U.S. law. The type of application and information required may differ according to the type of certificate requested and the commodity being exported. Exporters are urged to contact the appropriate center within the FDA for guidance on requesting procedures and export certificate eligibility for their particular country.

Contact: A general information document, *Guidance for Industry—FDA Export Certificates*, is available at *www.fda.gov/cber/gdlns/exprtcert.htm*. The FDA home page, *www.fda.gov*, also provides links to FDA centers. For certificates relating to drugs, call the Center for Drug Evaluation and Research at (301) 827-8983; for biologics, call the Center for Biologics Evaluation and Research at (301) 827-6201; for medical devices, call the Center for Devices and Radiological Health, Office of Compliance at (240) 276-0132; and for animal drugs, call the Center for Veterinary Medicine at (301) 827-0178.

Inspection Certificates for Food and Agricultural Exports, U.S. Department of Agriculture

Several agencies within U.S. Department of Agriculture (USDA) provide inspection services when certificates are required to clear imported products through overseas customs or are requested by foreign buyers.

Animal and Plant Health Inspection Service. The Animal and Plant Health Inspection Service (APHIS) provides exporters information on import and export requirements for plant and animal products and by-products. Phytosanitary inspections for plant materials are offered at ports and interior locations. Animal health certificates for animal products, including hides and pet foods, can be obtained from your local APHIS veterinarian.

Contact: For plant export certification, call (301) 734-8537. For animal health certification, call (301) 734-3277. For more information, visit the APHIS home page at *www.aphis.usda.gov*, and click on "Plant Health" and "Animal Health."

Federal Grain Inspection Service. The Federal Grain Inspection Service (FGIS) provides inspections under the U.S. Grain Standards Act and the Agricultural Marketing Act of 1946. FGIS also conducts mandatory inspections for all exported grain. Products examined by FGIS include rice, peas, beans, lentils, grains, and grain-based processed products.

Contact: For more information, call Robert Lijewski, Policies and Procedures Branch, at (202) 720-0224; fax (202) 720-1015; e-mail *robert.s.lijewski@usda.gov;* or visit *www.gipsa.usda.gov.*

Food Safety and Inspection Service. The Food Safety and Inspection Service (FSIS) guarantees that meat and poultry products are properly labeled and U.S. inspected and approved.

Contact: For more information on the FSIS, call (402) 221-7400, fax (402) 221-7479, or visit *www.fsis.usda.gov.*

Agricultural Marketing Service. The Agricultural Marketing Service (AMS), in cooperation with state agencies, offers official grading, inspection, and certification services; production and processing verification services; and chemical and microbiological testing services for a variety of agricultural products, including organic products. Grading, inspection, and certification services can be based on U.S. grade standards developed by the USDA for these products, or they can be based on applicant specifications and processes.

Contact: For more information about this voluntary food quality certification service, call Kenneth C. Clayton, associate administrator, AMS, at (202) 720-4276; fax (202) 720-8477; or e-mail *kenneth.clayton@usda.gov.* The AMS home page is *www.ams.usda.gov/AMSv1.0/.* AMS program areas include cotton, *www.ams.usda.gov/cotton;* dairy, *www.ams.usda.gov/dairy;* fruits and vegetables, *www.ams.usda.gov/fv;* poultry, *www.ams.usda.gov/poultry;* science and technology, *www.ams.usda.gov/science;* and tobacco, *www.ams.usda.gov/tobacco.* The AMS International Services home page is *www.ams.usda.gov/international.*

Seafood Inspection Program, National Oceanic and Atmospheric Administration, U.S. Department of Commerce. The National Oceanic and Atmospheric Administration (NOAA) Seafood Inspection Program includes consumer safety officers and trade specialists who offer a range of services to assist U.S. fishing industry businesses engaged in the export of fish and fishery products. Besides inspecting and certifying products for export, staff members advise seafood marketers about foreign regulations and maintain contact with foreign government regulatory agencies to resolve sanitary and hygienic issues. NOAA also promotes and facilitates the trade of U.S. fishery products internationally. The Seafood Inspection Program can verify, through on-site audits, that foreign processors meet U.S. Food and Drug Administration and U.S. Department of Commerce regulations governing the control of food safety hazards and sanitary hygienic conditions, including the construction and maintenance of facilities and equipment, processing techniques, and employee practices in the production of fishery products for human consumption.

Contact: For more information, call Kimberly Young, Seafood Inspection Program, at (800) 422-2750 or (301) 713-2355; fax (301) 713-1081; or visit *http://seafood.nmfs.noaa.gov.*

Environmental Technology Verification Program, U.S. Environmental Protection Agency. The Environmental Technology Verification (ETV) Program verifies the performance of innovative technologies that have the potential to improve protection of human health and the environment. ETV accelerates the entrance of new environmental technologies into the domestic and international marketplaces. Verified technologies are included for all environmental media—air, water, and land.

Contact: To learn more, visit the ETV home page at *www.epa.gov/etv.*

Wholesaler's Basic Permit, Alcohol and Tobacco Tax and Trade Bureau, U.S. Department of the Treasury. Exporters of wine, beer, and distilled spirits for resale in foreign commerce are required to obtain a federal wholesaler's basic permit from the Alcohol and Tobacco Tax and Trade Bureau (TTB), the agency that administers regulations relating to alcohol beverages and tobacco. A background check may be required before issuance of a wholesaler's basic permit. Producers that are in possession of a distilled spirits plant permit, brewer's notice, or winery permit may export under the authority of those documents and are not required to obtain the wholesaler's basic permit. Note that the foreign country may mandate specific documentation or additional permit requirements. Specialists at TTB can help companies navigate the application process and determine which foreign requirements, if any, apply.

Contact: To learn how to apply for a permit and to find more information on exporting beverage alcohol, call TTB's International Trade Division at (202) 927-8110, e-mail *itd@ttb. gov*, or visit *www.ttb.gov/itd*.

CHAPTER 10
EXPORT LICENSES AND CONTROLS

Bureau of Industry and Security, U.S. Department of Commerce

The mission of the Bureau of Industry and Security (BIS) is to advance U.S. national security, foreign policy, and economic objectives by ensuring an effective export control and treaty compliance system and promoting continued U.S. strategic technology leadership. BIS's activities include regulating the export and reexport of sensitive goods and technologies in an effective and efficient manner; enforcing export control, antiboycott, and public safety laws; cooperating with and assisting other countries on export control and strategic trade issues; helping U.S. industry comply with international arms control agreements; and monitoring the viability of the U.S. defense industrial base. BIS has an extensive Web site with information on export control policies and procedures. The bureau also has a staff available to counsel exporters; conduct export control seminars; and respond to inquiries from the exporting community regarding the Export Administration Regulations (EAR), export control policy, and licensing procedures. BIS plans, conducts, and participates in seminars, Webinars, online training, and other outreach efforts to help exporters understand and comply with the EAR.

Contact: For additional export control information and publications and related resources, including a new online Training Room, visit *www.bis.doc.gov*. To speak to an export counselor, call the Office of Exporter Services at (202) 482-4811 in Washington, D.C., or one of its two California locations at (949) 660-0144 in Newport Beach or at (408) 998-8806 in San Jose.

Office of Foreign Assets Control, U.S. Department of the Treasury

The Office of Foreign Assets Control (OFAC) administers and enforces economic and trade sanctions against targeted foreign countries, terrorists, and international narcotics traffickers and their agents in accordance with U.S. foreign policy and national security goals. OFAC publishes an extensive library of free materials on its Web site to help the international trade community comply with U.S. sanctions. The Web site includes summaries of sanctions programs by country and provides access to a guide titled *Foreign Assets Control Regulations for Exporters and Importers.* Also available is the "Specially Designated Nationals and Blocked Persons" list of entities and individuals with whom U.S. persons may not conduct business and whose property must be blocked if under the control of a U.S. person. Users can keep current with OFAC updates through a free subscription e-mail service. All of the information available on the Web site is also available through OFAC's free fax-on-demand service. OFAC also maintains a hotline staffed by compliance officers who are knowledgeable about international trade. They are available Monday through Friday (8:00 a.m. to 6:00 p.m. EST) to provide guidance on sanctions-related matters. The public also has the opportunity to provide comments or ask questions on OFAC's Web site.

Contact: To learn more, call the OFAC hotline at (800) 540-6322, or fax (202) 622-2426. The 24-hour fax-on-demand number is (202) 622-0077. The OFAC home page is *www.treas.gov/ofac.*

Directorate of Defense Trade Controls, U.S. Department of State

The Directorate of Defense Trade Controls administers Section 38 of the Arms Export Control Act and its implementing regulations, the International Traffic in Arms Regulations. It is responsible for regulating the export and brokering of U.S. defense articles, services, and related technical data covered by the U.S. Munitions List. The directorate, comprising three offices (Licensing, Compliance, and Policy), adjudicates arms export license applications and ensures export compliance in furtherance of U.S. national security and foreign policy objectives.

Contact: For more information, call the directorate's Response Team at (202) 663-1282, or visit *www.pmddtc.state.gov.*

APPENDIX A
EXPORT ASSISTANCE CENTER NETWORK

ALABAMA

Birmingham
950 22nd St. N., Rm. 707
Birmingham, AL 35203
Phone: (205) 731-1331
Fax: (205) 731-0076
E-mail: *office.birmingham@mail.doc.gov*

ALASKA

Anchorage
431 W. 7th Ave., Ste. 108
Anchorage, AK 99501
Phone: (907) 271-6237
Fax: (907) 271-6242
E-mail: *alaska.office.box@mail.doc.gov*

ARIZONA

Phoenix
1700 W. Washington St., Ste. 220
Phoenix, AZ 85007
Phone: (602) 640-2513
Fax: (602) 640-2518
E-mail: *phoenix.office.box@mail.doc.gov*

Tucson
120 N. Stone Ave., Ste. 200
Tucson, AZ 85701
Phone: (520) 670-5540
Fax: (520) 243-1910
E-mail: *tucson.office.box@mail.doc.gov*

ARKANSAS

Little Rock
425 W. Capitol Ave., Ste. 425
Little Rock, AR 72201
Phone: (501) 324-5794
Fax: (501) 324-7380
E-mail: *little.rock.office.box@mail.doc.gov*

CALIFORNIA

Bakersfield (Kern County)
2100 Chester Ave., 1st Fl., Ste. 166
Bakersfield, CA 93301
Phone: (661) 637-0136
Fax: (661) 637-0156
E-mail: *bakersfield.office.box@mail.doc.gov*

Fresno
550 E. Shaw Ave., Ste. 155
Fresno, CA 93710
Phone: (559) 227-6582
Fax: (559) 227-6509
E-mail: *fresno.office.box@mail.doc.gov*

Indio/Cabazon
Workforce Development Center
44-199 Monroe St., Ste. B308
Indio, CA 92201
Phone: (760) 342-1310
Fax: (760) 342-1565
E-mail: *cabazon.office.box@mail.doc.gov*

Inland Empire

2940 Inland Empire Blvd., Ste. 121
Ontario, CA 91764
Phone: (909) 466-4134
Fax: (909) 466-4140
E-mail: *ontariocal.office.box@mail.doc.gov*

Los Angeles (Downtown)

444 S. Flower St., 34th Fl.
Los Angeles, CA 90071
Phone: (213) 894-8784
Fax: (213) 894-8789
E-mail: *los.angeles.downtown.office.box@
mail.doc.gov*

Los Angeles (West)

11150 Olympic Blvd., Ste. 975
Los Angeles, CA 90064
Phone: (310) 235-7104
Fax: (310) 235-7220
E-mail: *los.angeles.office.box@mail.doc.gov*

Monterey

411 Pacific St., Ste. 316A
Monterey, CA 93940
Phone: (831) 641-9850
Fax: (831) 641-9849
E-mail: *montereyca.office.box@mail.doc.gov*

Newport Beach

3300 Irvine Ave., Ste. 305
Newport Beach, CA 92660
Phone: (949) 660-1688
Fax: (949) 660-1338
E-mail: *newport.beach.office.box@
mail.doc.gov*

Oakland

1301 Clay St., Ste. 630N
Oakland, CA 94612
Phone: (510) 273-7350
Fax: (510) 273-7352
E-mail: *oakland.office.box@mail.doc.gov*

Sacramento

1410 Ethan Way
Sacramento, CA 95825
Phone: (916) 566-7170
Fax: (916) 566-7123
E-mail: *sacramento.office.box@mail.doc.gov*

San Diego

6363 Greenwich Dr., Ste. 230
San Diego, CA 92122
Phone: (619) 557-5395
Fax: (619) 557-6176
E-mail: *san.diego.office.box@mail.doc.gov*

San Francisco

250 Montgomery St., 14th Fl.
San Francisco, CA 94104
Phone: (415) 705-2300
Fax: (415) 705-2299
E-mail: *san.francisco.office.box@
mail.doc.gov*

San Jose

55 S. Market St., Ste. 1040
San Jose, CA 95113
Phone: (408) 535-2757
Fax: (408) 535-2758
E-mail: *silicon.valley.office.box@mail.doc.gov*

San Rafael (North Bay/Novato)

50 Acacia Ave.
San Rafael, CA 94901
Phone: (415) 485-6200
Fax: (415) 485-6219
E-mail: *north.bay.office.box@mail.doc.gov*

Ventura County

333 Ponoma St.
Port Hueneme, CA 93041
Phone: (805) 488-4844
Fax: (805) 488-7801
E-mail: *ventura.office.box@mail.doc.gov*

COLORADO

Denver

World Trade Center
1625 Broadway, Ste. 680
Denver, CO 80202
Phone: (303) 844-6623
Fax: (303) 844-5651
E-mail: *denver.office.box@mail.doc.gov*

CONNECTICUT

Middletown

213 Court St., Ste. 903
Middletown, CT 06457
Phone: (860) 638-6950
Fax: (860) 638-6970
E-mail: *office.middletown@mail.doc.gov*

DELAWARE

Served by the Philadelphia,
Pennsylvania, U.S. Export
Assistance Center

DISTRICT OF COLUMBIA

Served by the Arlington, Virginia, U.S.
Export Assistance Center

FLORIDA

Clearwater

13805 58th St. N., Ste. 1-200
Clearwater, FL 33760
Phone: (727) 893-3738
Fax: (727) 893-3839
E-mail: *office.clearwater@mail.doc.gov*

Ft. Lauderdale

200 E. Las Olas Blvd., Ste. 1600
Ft. Lauderdale, FL 33301
Phone: (954) 356-6640
Fax: (954) 356-6644
E-mail: *office.ftlauderdale@mail.doc.gov*

Jacksonville

3 Independent Dr.
Jacksonville, FL 32202
Phone: (904) 232-1270
Fax: (904) 232-1271
E-mail: *jacksonville.office.box@*
        mail.doc.gov

Miami

5835 Blue Lagoon Dr., Ste. 203
Miami, FL 33126
Phone: (305) 526-7425
Fax: (305) 526-7434
E-mail: *office.miami@mail.doc.gov*

Orlando

315 E. Robinson St., Ste. 100
Orlando, FL 32801
Phone: (407) 648-6170
Fax: (407) 487-1909
E-mail: *office.orlando@mail.doc.gov*

Tallahassee

Atrium Building
325 John Knox Rd., Ste. 201
Tallahassee, FL 32303
Phone: (850) 942-9635
Fax: (850) 922-9595
E-mail: *tallahassee.office.box@
        mail.doc.gov*

GEORGIA

Atlanta

75 5th St. N.W., Ste. 1055
Atlanta, GA 30308
Phone: (404) 897-6090
Fax: (404) 897-6085
E-mail: *office.atlanta@mail.doc.gov*

Savannah

111 E. Liberty St., Ste. 202
Savannah, GA 31401
Phone: (912) 652-4204
Fax: (912) 652-4241
E-mail: *office.savannah@mail.doc.gov*

HAWAII AND THE PACIFIC ISLANDS

Honolulu

521 Ala Moana Blvd., Rm. 214
Honolulu, HI 96813
Phone: (808) 522-8040
Fax: (808) 522-8045
E-mail: *honolulu.office.box@mail.doc.gov*

IDAHO

Boise

700 W. State St., 2nd Fl.
Boise, ID 83720
Phone: (208) 364-7791
Fax: (208) 334-2783
E-mail: *boise.office.box@mail.doc.gov*

ILLINOIS

Chicago

200 W. Adams St., Ste. 2450
Chicago, IL 60606
Phone: (312) 353-8040
Fax: (312) 353-8120
E-mail: *chicago.office.box@mail.doc.gov*

Libertyville

28055 Ashley Cir., Ste. 212
Libertyville, IL 60048
Phone: (847) 327-9082
Fax: (847) 247-0423
E-mail: *libertyville.office.box@mail.doc.gov*

Bradley University
Jobst Hall, Rm. 141
922 N. Glenwood Ave.
Peoria, IL 61606
Phone: (309) 671-7815
Fax: (309) 671-7818
E-mail: *peoria.office.box@mail.doc.gov*

EIGERlab
605 Fulton Ave., Ste. E103
Rockford, IL 61103
Phone: (815) 316-2380
Fax: (888) 628-2571
E-mail: *rockford.office.box@mail.doc.gov*

INDIANA

11405 N. Pennsylvania St., Ste. 106
Carmel, IN 46032
Phone: (317) 582-2300
Fax: (317) 582-2301
E-mail: *office.indianapolis@mail.doc.gov*

IOWA

210 Walnut St., Rm. 749
Des Moines, IA 50309
Phone: (515) 284-4590
Fax: (515) 288-1437
E-mail: *des.moines.office.box@mail.doc.gov*

KANSAS

150 N. Main St., Ste. 200
Wichita, KS 67202
Phone: (316) 263-4067
Fax: (316) 263-8306
E-mail: *wichita.office.box@mail.doc.gov*

KENTUCKY

333 W. Vine St., Ste. 1600
Lexington, KY 40507
Phone: (859) 225-7001
Fax: (859) 201-1139
E-mail: *sara.moreno@mail.doc.gov*

601 W. Broadway, Rm. 634B
Louisville, KY 40202
Phone: (502) 582-5066
Fax: (502) 582-6573
E-mail: *office.louisville@mail.doc.gov*

LOUISIANA

2 Canal St., Ste. 2710
New Orleans, LA 70130
Phone: (504) 589-6546
Fax: (504) 589-2337
E-mail: *new.orleans.office.box@
mail.doc.gov*

Shreveport

Business Education Building 119H
LSUS-One University Pl.
Shreveport, LA 71115
Phone: (318) 676-3064
Fax: (318) 676-3063
E-mail: *shreveport.office.box@mail.doc.gov*

MAINE

Portland

Maine International Trade Center
511 Congress St.
Portland, ME 04101
Phone: (207) 541-7430
Fax: (207) 541-7420
E-mail: *office.portlandME@mail.doc.gov*

MARYLAND

Baltimore

300 W. Pratt St., Ste. 300
Baltimore, MD 21201
Phone: (410) 962-4539
Fax: (410) 962-4529
E-mail: *office.baltimoreusec@mail.doc.gov*

MASSACHUSETTS

Boston

JFK Federal Building
55 New Sudbury St., Ste. 1826A
Boston, MA 02203
Phone: (617) 565-4301
Fax: (617) 565-4313
E-mail: *office.boston@mail.doc.gov*

MICHIGAN

Detroit

8109 E. Jefferson Ave., Ste. 110
Detroit, MI 48214
Phone: (313) 226-3650
Fax: (313) 226-3657
E-mail: *office.detroit@mail.doc.gov*

Grand Rapids

401 W. Fulton St., Ste. 349C
Grand Rapids, MI 49504
Phone: (616) 458-3564
Fax: (616) 458-3872
E-mail: *office.grandrapids@mail.doc.gov*

Pontiac

250 Elizabeth Lake Rd., Ste. 1300 W.
Pontiac, MI 48341
Phone: (248) 975-9600
Fax: (248) 975-9606
E-mail: *office.pontiac@mail.doc.gov*

Ypsilanti

Eastern Michigan University
300 W. Michigan Ave., Ste. 306G
Ypsilanti, MI 48197
Phone: (734) 487-0259
Fax: (734) 485-2396
E-mail: *ypsilanti.office.box@mail.doc.gov*

MINNESOTA

Minneapolis

100 N. 6th St., Ste. 210-C
Minneapolis, MI 55403
Phone: (612) 348-1638
Fax: (612) 348-1650
E-mail: *minneapolis.office.box@mail.doc.gov*

MISSISSIPPI

Mississippi

175 E. Capitol St., Ste. 255
Jackson, MS 39201
Phone: (601) 965-4130
Fax: (601) 965-4132
E-mail: *jackson.office.box@mail.doc.gov*

MISSOURI

Kansas City

2509 Commerce Tower
911 Main St.
Kansas City, MO 64105
Phone: (816) 421-1876
Fax: (816) 471-7839
E-mail: *kansas.city.office.box@mail.doc.gov*

St. Louis

8235 Forsyth Blvd., Ste. 520
St. Louis, MO 63105
Phone: (314) 425-3302
Fax: (314) 425-3381
E-mail: *st.louis.office.box@mail.doc.gov*

MONTANA

Missoula

University of Montana
Gallagher Business Building, Ste. 257
Missoula, MT 59812
Phone: (406) 542-6656
Fax: (406) 542-6659
E-mail: *montana.office.box@mail.doc.gov*

NEBRASKA

Omaha

13006 W. Center Rd.
Omaha, NE 68144
Phone: (402) 597-0193
Fax: (402) 595-1194
E-mail: *omaha.office.box@mail.doc.gov*

NEVADA

Las Vegas

400 S. 4th St., Ste. 250
Las Vegas, NV 89101
Phone: (702) 388-6694
Fax: (702) 388-6469
E-mail: *las.vegas.office.box@mail.doc.gov*

Reno

1 E. 1st St., 16th Fl.
Reno, NV 89501
Phone: (775) 784-5203
Fax: (775) 784-5343
E-mail: *reno.office.box@mail.doc.gov*

NEW HAMPSHIRE

Portsmouth

17 New Hampshire Ave.
Portsmouth, NH 03801
Phone: (603) 334-6074
Fax: (603) 334-6110
E-mail: *office.portsmouth@mail.doc.gov*

NEW JERSEY

Newark

744 Broad St., Ste. 1505
Newark, NJ 07102
Phone: (973) 645-4682
Fax: (973) 645-4783
E-mail: *office.newark@mail.doc.gov*

Trenton

20 W. State St.
P.O. Box 820
Trenton, NJ 08625
Phone: (609) 989-2100
Fax: (609) 989-2395
E-mail: *office.trenton@mail.doc.gov*

NEW MEXICO

Santa Fe

New Mexico Dept. of Economic
    Development
P.O. Box 20003
1100 St. Francis Dr. (use for courier service)
Santa Fe, NM 87504
Phone: (505) 231-0075
Fax: (505) 827-0211
E-mail: *santa.fe.office.box@mail.doc.gov*

NEW YORK

Buffalo

130 S. Elmwood Ave., Ste. 530
Buffalo, NY 14202
Phone: (716) 551-4191
Fax: (716) 551-5290
E-mail: *office.buffalo@mail.doc.gov*

Harlem

163 W. 125th St., Ste. 901
New York, NY 10027
Phone: (212) 860-6200
Fax: (212) 860-6203
E-mail: *office.harlem@mail.doc.gov*

Long Island

Serviced by the New York U.S. Export
    Assistance Center
33 Whitehall St., 22nd Fl.
New York, NY 10004
Phone: (212) 809-2682
Fax: (212) 809-2687
E-mail: *office.longisland@mail.doc.gov*

New York

33 Whitehall St., 22nd Fl.
New York, NY 10004
Phone: (212) 809-2675
Fax: (212) 809-2687
E-mail: *office.newyork@mail.doc.gov*

Rochester

400 Andrews St., Ste. 710
Rochester, NY 14604
Phone: (585) 263-6480
Fax: (585) 325-6505
E-mail: *erin.cole@mail.doc.gov*

Westchester

707 Westchester Ave., Ste. 209
White Plains, NY 10604
Phone: (914) 682-6712
Fax: (914) 682-6698
E-mail: *office.westchester@mail.doc.gov*

NORTH CAROLINA

Charlotte

521 E. Morehead St., Ste. 435
Charlotte, NC 28202
Phone: (704) 333-4886
Fax: (704) 332-2681
E-mail: *office.charlotte@mail.doc.gov*

Greensboro

342 N. Elm St.
Greensboro, NC 27401
Phone: (336) 333-5345
Fax: (336) 333-5158
E-mail: *office.greensboro@mail.doc.gov*

Raleigh

10900 World Trade Blvd., Ste. 110
Raleigh, NC 27617
Phone: (919) 281-2750
Fax: (919) 281-2754
E-mail: *office.raleigh@mail.doc.gov*

NORTH DAKOTA

Fargo

51 Broadway, Ste. 505
Fargo, ND 58102
Phone: (701) 239-5080
Fax: (701) 237-9734
E-mail: *northdakota.office.box@*
mail.doc.gov

OHIO

Akron

Kent State University, Administrative
   Services Building
Kent, OH 44242
Phone: (330) 678-0695
E-mail: *todd.hiser@mail.doc.gov*

Cincinnati

36 E. 7th St., Ste. 2650
Cincinnati, OH 45202
Phone: (513) 684-2944
Fax: (513) 684-3227
E-mail: *office.cincinnati@mail.doc.gov*

Cleveland

600 Superior Ave. E., Ste. 700
Cleveland, OH 44114
Phone: (216) 522-4750
Fax: (216) 522-2235
E-mail: *office.cleveland@mail.doc.gov*

Columbus

401 N. Front St., Ste. 200
Columbus, OH 43215
Phone: (614) 365-9510
Fax: (614) 365-9598
E-mail: *office.columbus@mail.doc.gov*

Toledo

300 Madison Ave., Ste. 270
Toledo, OH 43604
Phone: (419) 241-0683
Fax: (419) 241-0684
E-mail: *office.toledo@mail.doc.gov*

OKLAHOMA

Oklahoma City

301 N.W. 63rd St., Ste. 330
Oklahoma City, OK 73116
Phone: (405) 608-5302
Fax: (405) 608-4211
E-mail: *oklahomacity.office.box@
    mail.doc.gov*

Tulsa

700 N. Greenwood Ave., Ste. 1400
Tulsa, OK 74106
Phone: (918) 581-7650
Fax: (918) 581-6263
E-mail: *tulsa.office.box@mail.doc.gov*

OREGON

Portland

One World Trade Center
121 S.W. Salmon St., Ste. 242
Portland, OR 97204
Phone: (503) 326-3001
Fax: (503) 326-6351
E-mail: *portlandor.office.box@mail.doc.gov*

PENNSYLVANIA

Harrisburg

Millersville University
Office of International Affairs
2 S. George St., Cumberland House
P.O. Box 40
Millersville, PA 17551
Phone: (717) 872-4386
Fax: (717) 871-2132
E-mail: *office.harrisburg@mail.doc.gov*

Philadelphia

Curtis Center, Ste. 580 W.
Independence Square W.
601 Walnut St.
Philadelphia, PA 19106
Phone: (215) 597-6101
Fax: (215) 597-6123
E-mail: *office.philadelphia@mail.doc.gov*

Pittsburgh

425 6th Ave., Ste. 2950
Pittsburgh, PA 15219
Phone: (412) 644-2800
Fax: (412) 644-2803
E-mail: *office.pittsburgh@mail.doc.gov*

PUERTO RICO

San Juan

Centro Internacional de Mercadeo Torre II,
    Ste. 702
Guaynabo, PR 00968
Phone: (787) 775-1992
Fax: (787) 781-7178
E-mail: *office.sanjuanpr@mail.doc.gov*

RHODE ISLAND

Providence

315 Iron Horse Way, Ste. 101
Providence, RI 02908
Phone: (401) 528-5104
Fax: (401) 528-5067
E-mail: *office.providence@mail.doc.gov*

SOUTH CAROLINA

Charleston

1362 McMillan Ave., Ste. 100
N. Charleston, SC 29405
Phone: (843) 746-3404
Fax: (843) 529-0305
E-mail: *phil.minard@mail.doc.gov*

Columbia

Midlands Technical College
7300 College St., Harbison Hall, 2nd Fl.
Irmo, SC 29063
Phone: (803) 732-5211
Fax: (803) 732-5241
E-mail: *office.columbia@mail.doc.gov*

Greenville

Greenville Technical College
Buck Mickel Center
216 S. Pleasantburg Dr., Ste. 243
Greenville, SC 29607
Phone: (864) 250-8429
Fax: (864) 250-6729
E-mail: *office.greenville@mail.doc.gov*

SOUTH DAKOTA

Sioux Falls

Augustana College
2001 S. Summit Ave., Madsen Center, Rm. 122
Sioux Falls, SD 57197
Phone: (605) 330-4264
Fax: (605) 330-4266
E-mail: *sioux.falls.office.box@mail.doc.gov*

TENNESSEE

Knoxville

17 Market Sq., Ste. 201
Knoxville, TN 37902
Phone: (865) 545-4637
Fax: (865) 545-4435
E-mail: *knoxville.office.box@mail.doc.gov*

Memphis

22 N. Front St., Ste. 200
Memphis, TN 38103
Phone: (901) 544-0930
Fax: (901) 543-3510
E-mail: *office.memphis@mail.doc.gov*

Nashville

Tennessee Tower
312 8th Ave. N., 10th Fl.
Nashville, TN 37423
Phone: (615) 736-2222
Fax: (615) 736-2226
E-mail: *office.nashville@mail.doc.gov*

TEXAS

Austin

221 E. 11th St., 4th Fl.
Austin, TX 78701
Mailing: P.O. Box 12428
Austin, TX 78711
Phone: (512) 916-5939
Fax: (512) 916-5940
E-mail: *austin.office.box@mail.doc.gov*

Ft. Worth

808 Throckmorton St.
Ft. Worth, TX 76102
Phone: (817) 392-2673
Fax: (817) 392-2668
E-mail: *fort.worth.office.box@mail.doc.gov*

Houston

1919 Smith St., Ste. 1026
Houston, TX 77002
Phone: (713) 209-3104
Fax: (713) 209-3135
E-mail: *houston.office.box@mail.doc.gov*

North Texas

1450 Hughes Rd., Ste. 220
Grapevine, TX 76051
Phone: (817) 310-3744
Fax: (817) 310-3757
E-mail: *north.texas.office.box@mail.doc.gov*

San Antonio

203 S. St. Mary's St., Ste. 360
San Antonio, TX 78205
Phone: (210) 228-9878
Fax: (210) 228-9874
E-mail: *san.antonio.office.box@*
mail.doc.gov

South Texas

6401 S. 36th St., Ste. 4
McAllen, TX 78503
Phone: (956) 661-0238
Fax: (956) 661-0239
E-mail: *south.texas.office.box@*
mail.doc.gov

West Texas

1400 N. FM 1788, Rm. 1303
Midland, TX 79707
Phone: (432) 552-2490
Fax: (432) 552-3490
E-mail: *west.texas.office.box@mail.doc.gov*

UTAH

Salt Lake City

9690 S. 300 W., Ste. 201D
Sandy, UT 84070
Phone: (801) 255-1871
Fax: (801) 255-3147
E-mail: *salt.lake.city.office.box@mail.doc.gov*

VERMONT

Montpelier

National Life Building, 6th Fl.
Montpelier, VT 05620
Phone: (802) 828-4508
Fax: (802) 828-3258
E-mail: *office.montpelier@mail.doc.gov*

VIRGINIA

Arlington (Northern Virginia)

1100 N. Glebe Rd., Ste. 1500
Arlington, VA 22201
Phone: (703) 235-0331
Fax: (703) 524-2649
E-mail: *office.nova@mail.doc.gov*

Richmond

400 N. 8th St., Ste. 412
P.O. Box 10026
Richmond, VA 23240
Phone: (804) 771-2246
Fax: (804) 771-2390
E-mail: *office.richmond@mail.doc.gov*

WASHINGTON

Seattle

2601 4th Ave., Ste. 320
Seattle, WA 98121
Phone: (206) 553-5615
Fax: (206) 553-7253
E-mail: *seattle.office.box@mail.doc.gov*

Spokane

Spokane Regional Chamber of Commerce
801 W. Riverside, Ste. 100
Spokane, WA 99201
Phone: (509) 353-2625
Fax: (509) 353-2449
E-mail: *spokane.office.box@mail.doc.gov*

WEST VIRGINIA

Charleston

1116 Smith St., Ste. 302
Charleston, WV 25301
Phone: (304) 347-5123
Fax: (304) 347-5408
E-mail: *charlestonwv.office.box@*
      mail.doc.gov

Wheeling

Wheeling Jesuit University
316 Washington Ave.
Wheeling, WV 26003
Phone: (304) 243-5493
Fax: (304) 243-5494
E-mail: *office.wheeling@mail.doc.gov*

WISCONSIN

Milwaukee

517 E. Wisconsin Ave., Rm. 596
Milwaukee, WI 53202
Phone: (414) 297-3473
Fax: (414) 297-3470
E-mail: *milwaukee.office.box@mail.doc.gov*

WYOMING

Served by the Denver, Colorado, U.S.
Export Assistance Center

APPENDIX B

TRADE PROMOTION COORDINATING COMMITTEE AGENCIES
AND ADDRESSES

U.S. Department of Commerce
1401 Constitution Avenue, NW
Washington, DC 20230
www.commerce.gov

U.S. Department of State
2201 C Street, NW
Washington, DC 20520
www.state.gov

U.S. Department of the Treasury
1500 Pennsylvania Avenue, NW
Washington, DC 20220
www.treasury.gov

U.S. Department of Defense
The Pentagon
Washington, DC 20301
www.defense.gov

U.S. Department of the Interior
1849 C Street, NW
Washington, DC 20240
www.interior.gov

U.S. Department of Agriculture
14th Street and Independence Avenue, SW
Washington, DC 20250
www.usda.gov

U.S. Department of Labor
200 Constitution Avenue, NW
Washington, DC 20210
www.dol.gov

U.S. Department of Transportation
400 7th Street, SW
Washington, DC 20590
www.transportation.gov

U.S. Department of Energy
1000 Independence Avenue, SW
Washington, DC 20585
www.energy.gov

Office of Management and Budget
New Executive Office Building
725 17th Street, NW
Washington, DC 20503
www.omb.gov

Office of the United States Trade Representative
600 17th Street, NW
Washington, DC 20508
www.ustr.gov

Council of Economic Advisers
Eisenhower Executive Office Building, Room 99
The White House
Washington, DC 20502
www.whitehouse.gov/cea

Environmental Protection Agency
Ronald Reagan Building, Room 31237
1300 Pennsylvania Avenue, NW
Washington, DC 20460
www.epa.gov

U.S. Small Business Administration
409 3rd Street, SW
Washington, DC 20416
www.sba.gov

U.S. Agency for International Development
State Department Building
320 21st Street, NW
Washington, DC 20523
www.usaid.gov

Export–Import Bank of the United States
811 Vermont Avenue, NW
Washington, DC 20571
www.exim.gov

Overseas Private Investment Corporation
1100 New York Avenue, NW
Washington, DC 20527
www.opic.gov

U.S. Trade and Development Agency
1000 Wilson Boulevard, Suite 1600
Arlington, VA 22209
www.ustda.gov

National Economic Council
The White House
Washington, DC 20502
www.whitehouse.gov/nec

U.S. Department of Homeland Security
Washington, DC 20528
www.dhs.gov

ALPHABETICAL LIST OF PROGRAMS

ACRONYMS AND ABBREVIATIONS

AD	antidumping
AGRICOLA	Agricultural Online Access database
AMS	Agricultural Marketing Service
APHIS	Animal and Plant Health Inspection Service
BIC	Business Information Center
BIS	Bureau of Industry and Security
CCC	Commodity Credit Corporation
CCG	Country Commercial Guide
CMR	customized market research
CS	U.S. Commercial Service
CVD	countervailing duty
DEC	District Export Council
EAR	Export Administration Regulations
EDN	Enterprise Development Network
ELAN	Export Legal Assistance Network
EMP	Emerging Markets Program
ERS	Economic Research Service
ETV	Environmental Technology Verification
EU	European Union
EWCP	Export Working Capital Program
Ex–Im	Export–Import
FAS	Foreign Agricultural Service
FCIB	Finance, Credit, and International Business
FDA	Food and Drug Administration
FGIS	Federal Grain Inspection Service
FGP	Facility Guarantee Program
FLT	*Foreign Labor Trends*
FMD	Foreign Market Development
FSIS	Food Safety and Inspection Service
FSO	foreign service officer
FUSE	Featured U.S. Exporters
IBC	India Business Center
ICP	International Company Profile
IDB	International Data Base
IPS	International Partner Search
ITA	International Trade Administration
MAC	Market Access and Compliance

MAP	Market Access Program
MAS	Manufacturing and Services
MBDA	Minority Business Development Agency
MBEC	Minority Business Enterprise Center
MDB	multilateral development bank
MDCP	Market Development Cooperator Program
MENA	Middle East and North Africa
MEP	Manufacturing Extension Partnership
MSMEs	micro, small, and medium-sized enterprises
NABEC	Native American Business Enterprise Center
NAFTA	North American Free Trade Agreement
NAL	National Agricultural Library
NCSCI	National Center for Standards and Certification Information
NIST	National Institute of Standards and Technology
NOAA	National Oceanic and Atmospheric Administration
NTIS	National Technical Information Service
OECD	Organization for Economic Cooperation and Development
OFAC	Office of Foreign Assets Control
OIT	Office of International Trade
OPIC	Overseas Private Investment Corporation
OTEXA	Office of Textiles and Apparel
OTII	Office of Trade and Industry Information
SABIT	Special American Business Internship Training
SBA	U.S. Small Business Administration
SBDC	Small Business Development Center
SBIC	small business investment company
SCORE	Service Corps of Retired Executives
SRTG	State Regional Trade Group
STOP!	Strategy Targeting Organized Piracy
TCC	Trade Compliance Center
TIC	Trade Information Center
TTB	Tax and Trade Bureau
USDA	U.S. Department of Agriculture
USEAC	U.S. Export Assistance Center
USTDA	U.S. Trade and Development Agency
USTR	Office of the United States Trade Representative
WTO	World Trade Organization

www.ingramcontent.com/pod-product-compliance
Lightning Source LLC
Chambersburg PA
CBHW081836170526
45167CB00007B/2827